Fearless

STORIES OF THE
American
Saints

Alice Camille and Paul Boudreau
Original illustrations by Thomas Hann

Franciscan
MEDIA
Cincinnati, Ohio

Scripture passages have been taken from *New Revised Standard Version Bible*, copyright ©1989 by the Division of Christian Education of the National Council of the Churches of Christ in the U.S.A., and used by permission. All rights reserved.

Cover and book design by Mark Sullivan
Cover image © Argus | Fotolia

LIBRARY OF CONGRESS CATALOGING-IN-PUBLICATION DATA
Camille, Alice L.
Fearless : stories of the American saints / Alice Camille and Paul Boudreau; original illustrations by Thomas Hann.
pages cm
Includes bibliographical references.
ISBN 978-1-61636-637-7 (alk. paper)
1. Christian saints—United States—Biography. 2. United States—Church history. I. Title.
BX4659.U6C36 2014
282.092'273—dc23
[B]
2014019208

ISBN 978-1-61636-637-7

Copyright ©2014, Alice Camille and Paul Boudreau. Illustrations copyright ©2014, Thomas Hann. All rights reserved.

Published by Franciscan Media
28 W. Liberty St.
Cincinnati, OH 45202
www.FranciscanMedia.org

Printed in the United States of America.
Printed on acid-free paper.
14 15 16 17 18 5 4 3 2 1

Contents

INTRODUCTION | *vii*

PART ONE | *1*
Saints in America: Their Context and Contribution

PART TWO | *21*
Biographies of the American Saints

CHAPTER ONE | *23*
Isaac Jogues (1607–1646), René Goupil (1608–1642), and Jean de Lalande (d. 1646): Missionary Heroes of the New World

CHAPTER TWO | *35*
Kateri Tekakwitha: The Lily of the Mohawks (1656–1680)

CHAPTER THREE | *47*
Blessed Junípero (Miguel José) Serra: Father of the California Missions (1713–1784)

CHAPTER FOUR | *57*
Elizabeth Ann Bayley Seton: The Family Saint (1774–1821)

CHAPTER FIVE | *69*
Rose-Philippine Duchesne: The Woman Who Prays Always (1769–1852)

CHAPTER SIX | *85*
Theodore (Anne-Thérèse) Guérin: Pioneer Educator and Peacemaker (1798–1856)

CHAPTER SEVEN | *101*
John Nepomucene Neumann: The Little Bishop That Could (1811–1860)

CHAPTER EIGHT | *117*
Blessed Francis Xavier Seelos: The Happy Healer (1819–1867)

CHAPTER NINE | *131*
Damien (Joseph) de Veuster: The Face of Christ at Molokai (1840–1889)

CHAPTER TEN | *143*
Marianne (Barbara Koob) Cope: Angel of Mercy to the Sick (1838–1918)

CHAPTER ELEVEN | *159*
Frances Xavier (Maria Francesca) Cabrini: Teacher of the Heart (1850–1917)

CHAPTER TWELVE | *173*
Katharine (Catherine Mary) Drexel: America's Promise Keeper (1858–1955)

EPILOGUE | *195*

BIBLIOGRAPHY | *199*

*In grateful memory of Dale K. Gilson,
layman, seeker, holy man, friend—
one of many uncanonized saints
this country has produced.*

Note to Readers

All of the individuals chronicled in these pages lived in centuries that did not share our sensitive appreciation of racial and cultural differences. Native Americans were originally mistaken as "Indians" by explorers seeking a western route to India. Native peoples in every land were routinely described as "savages" by colonizing forces bearing European standards of civilization. African Americans, brought to this country to serve as slaves, were termed "Negros" in the politest of racial conversations, and "Colored" more commonly. There were many worse categorizations for both groups, as well as for every ethnic distinction in American society. Catholics themselves were Popish or papists and more. To represent the history of the times accurately, this book occasionally uses terms from another era. It is not our intention to offend or disparage anyone in so doing.

Introduction

You would think writing a book about American saints would be a simple matter: tell inspiring stories of noteworthy lives. Classic works like Alban Butler's *Lives of the Saints* provide a calendar of shimmering biographies tinged with miracles to make the reader ponder and marvel.

In the course of our reading and conversations, however, it became apparent that our saints are not like the traditional superheroes of the faith we're accustomed to reading about. For one thing, they mostly lived and labored in a single compressed area: the North American continent. They also inhabited relatively modern times: the fistful of centuries known as American history. These lives, then, are not diffused by legend. Most are, in fact, meticulously documented, photographed, and available for inspection.

More than that, the similarities and avenues of interconnection between these dozen or so biographies soon became its own story. These men and women revealed themselves, not just as discreet and interesting characters, but more like one seamless story of American Catholicism. They passed through many of the same landmark institutions (Mothers Elizabeth Ann Seton and Theodore Guérin found a touchstone at St. Peter's Church in New York; Guérin and Rose-Philippine Duchesne were both nursed through illnesses at the Ursuline convent in New Orleans); encountered each other (Katharine Drexel and Frances Cabrini shared advice about dealing with Rome; John Nepomucene Neumann and Francis Xavier Seelos lived together in Pittsburgh); had the same allies in bishops or patrons (Seton's best friend became Guérin's recruiting bishop; another Seton supporter later drafted Duchesne); or literally passed the baton to each other (Father Damien de Veuster bequeathed his afflicted community to Mother Marianne Cope).

The work begun by the Jesuit martyrs and Junípero Serra became the life's work, two centuries later, of Katharine Drexel. Mohawk Kateri Tekakwitha was born in the town where the Jesuit missionaries died—and all share a shrine today. Cities like New Orleans were familiar stomping grounds for Seelos, Cabrini, Drexel, Guérin, and Duchesne. Baltimore was a place most of them knew from personal experience. All embraced similar goals as teachers, leaders, healers, and exemplary pillars of faith.

Through the stories of figures the Church has recognized as holy, a larger story of a distinctly American way of holiness begins to emerge. That is what this book is about. We explore this history in several ways, which we hope will be persuasive of the remarkable unity of American Catholic sanctity. In the first section, we offer an overview of our national history, and how the saints fit into the weave of it. In the next section, we present individual portraits of canonized and beatified Americans whose humanity feels very close to us because they are, across the centuries, our neighbors.

Throughout the book we insert timelines, sayings, and contemporary updates to contextualize and animate these histories. We hope this story unveils a window of possibility through which to view how all of us might find our place among these heroic hearts. For this generation, too, must produce its saints.

Part One

Saints in America:
Their Context and Contribution

What is a saint? We are tempted to reply at once: "a very holy person." Ah, but what is holiness? That is a more complex issue. We can't point to a foolproof lifestyle to define what holiness is supposed to look like. Some canonized saints of the Church were kings and queens in palaces; others begged on the streets of their cities. Some were wellborn and educated, while as many were peasants, unsuccessful students, or simpleminded.

Some saints ranked among the popes, bishops, priests, and religious; others were farmers, doorkeepers, parents, even children. Some prayed and wrote in solemn cloisters; others wandered the countryside preaching. Some performed miracles, and many others are remembered for great wisdom or compassion. More than a few were martyred by methods artists have rendered in magnificent horror to impress such tremendous love and sacrifice upon the religious imagination. Others died of old age in their beds, with loved ones gathered around them.

Those of us who grew up with images of saints encircling our spiritual sensibilities are impressed above all by a certain mythic quality endowing these figures. They seem to exist without the temporal anchor that weighs heavily on the rest of us. In their soulful union with God, saints appear to float above history and its gritty concerns. We may be hard pressed to locate most of these sacred personalities on the globe, or to pin them down to a particular generation. We know them, rather, from their writings or what others have said about them. For the most part, the average saint remains locked in a timeless vacuum of plaster, stained glass, holy card, and legend. He or she, frankly, is not of this world, unlike the rest of us.

A wrench gets thrown into the mythmaking process once the element of proximity is added to the mix. The hometown celebrity can never quite escape the history of having been the ponytailed girl in algebra class or the young man who mowed lawns. Locality and familiarity make the saints of the United States most striking for those of us anchored in the soil of this country and its uniquely experimental history. The shiny surreal saints we grew up with—faraway figures from places like Assisi, Avila, Padua, or Hippo—seem to have inhabited the celestial communion forever. We have largely lost them behind a haze of *hagiography*, which means "idealizing or idolizing biography." Our homegrown saints are different. They share a story we have heard from secular history books. The U.S. saints step (and sometimes stumble) out of the pages of that history, traveling territory we know by heart as citizens of these same neighborhoods.

In their remarkable proximity to us, the saints of this country are reminders that all saints really do start on the ground: in some city or village, among a particular people, bearing the values and ideas of their generations. From their precise perch in time, there is information they don't have, or perspectives they can't imagine, that will seem flatly apparent in future centuries. Wrapped in threadbare mortality, each has flaws that become part of the lumber of their sanctification. The saints of our land drop anchor in the common cultural waters that are still in the process of shaping us. This makes their stories especially relevant as we seek a way of holiness for ourselves.

Making intercession through the saints is a time-honored tradition among Catholics. We might well utilize the special graces of these women and men who achieved sanctity by sweat and tears—and sometimes blood—on these shores. But the goal of this book isn't to present more holy lives to admire, nor to add to our chain of heavenly advocates. We can be sure no saint purposefully aimed to be canonized, or sought to be the object of veneration and prayers! These American lives are uniquely offered for our contemplation—to imitate their motivations if not always their methods—so that we too might be numbered among the holy ones in our own time.

What Makes a Saint American?

It is important to define our term. What do we mean by an American saint? The history of the United States officially begins in 1776, but the colonial era predates that year by three centuries. This means some "U.S." saints labored and died here before the story of our nation properly began. In the seventeenth century, three of the eight Jesuit martyrs of North America—Isaac Jogues, René Goupil, and Jean de Lalande—died as French citizens in what is now U.S. territory. Mohawk tribeswoman Kateri Tekakwitha, sharing the time frame of the Jesuits, was not a citizen of the U.S.

Beatified Franciscan Junípero Serra marched up the West Coast founding missions before the establishment of the new nation. Known as California's founding father, Serra was doing it all for the glory of God and Spain. Even Elizabeth Ann Seton, born in New York, was a subject of the British Empire and only became a U.S. citizen when the ground under her feet changed hands as a result of the Revolutionary War.

Other holy figures who are identified with their accomplishments in our nation were not born in the U.S., although many did gain citizenship later: Mother Frances Xavier Cabrini was Italian-born, Bishop John Neumann was from Bohemia, Mothers Philippine Duchesne and Theodore Guérin were both French, Father Damien de Veuster was from Belgium, and Mother Marianne Cope and beatified Redemptorist Francis Xavier Seelos were both German.

In addition, it must be remembered that what constituted the United States was in flux throughout these centuries. If the Jesuit martyrs and Tekakwitha lived before "The Star-Spangled Banner" was ever conceived, Serra died in a California that would not be incorporated into the U.S. story for some time to come. Father Damien ministered at Molokai on the so-called Sandwich Islands that did not yet belong to the U.S. as our fiftieth state.

In these early decades of the twenty-first century, the only American-born U.S. citizen to be Canonized: to date is Mother Katharine Drexel of Philadelphia. It would be a strangely picky piety that would draw the line at Drexel's feet and proclaim her the only "real" U.S. saint.

Rooted in History, Grounded in Faith
Presented in the following chapters are the stories of intriguing lives that merited canonization or beatification from within the scope of American territory. We hope these stories will open the door to a discussion of distinctly American traits that add something to the story of Catholicism that is not prominent in old-world saints or at earlier times.

Also within the scope of this effort is the desire to tell these stories within the context of our unique cultural history. These were, after all, men and women who walked the streets of New York, Philadelphia, and Baltimore; who worked in New Orleans, Denver, and along California's coast. They penetrated the heartland of Indiana and Missouri with missions and churches, schools and hospitals. They preached in the Southwest and brought hope to island territories that would later become part of our national story.

The implications of a common geography are remarkable in a country so young. These American saints were deeply affected by the currents that shaped the world we U.S. citizens inhabit today. Since 1492, the formidable movements of empires—Spain, France, and England—indelibly impressed upon the cultures of Florida, California, and the Southwest, the lands of the Louisiana Purchase, and the first thirteen colonies of the Eastern seaboard a character and culture, architecture, and attitude still imprinted on these areas. The ways in which these vast areas changed hands left their legacies—some more bitter than others. Our future saints lived in the midst of these conflicts and bore the burdens of working in such difficult times.

When wars were fought—Revolutionary or Civil, Spanish-American or world-encompassing—our saints were as personally impacted by the outcomes as any of us would have been. And when government,

Church, or other powers acted from the dark motives of greed and personal ambition, or out of ignorance, disordered zeal, or prejudice, these Catholic men and women struggled within the framework of such authorities and times to seek a brighter and better course.

Modern readers are tempted to judge the actors on history's stage in the glaring light of contemporary understanding, often forgetting the participants' original context. If we view every saint in the Church's canon by present-day standards, many come up wanting in some measure. At the same time, some saints who were viewed quite badly within their own generations develop improved profiles in the rearview mirror.

In matters of race and gender, slavery and privilege, clergy and laity, interfaith and ecumenical relations, labor and management, the story of our country contains bleak and shameful chapters that are hard to own. We want to look the other way, as we would in the presence of an indelicacy. The lives of the saints do not permit this, and these lovers of truth would not ask this of us, even if such inspection reflected poorly on them. They engaged hard questions within their social context, and might not flinch if we ask similar questions of them from the privileged perspective of a later century. If we can learn from their errors as much as from their fervor, their usefulness as examples in faith is doubled. If we can forgive past generations for the limits of their understanding, maybe future generations will forgive us our equally time-bound smugness.

Few of us can guess now what certitudes will be available to the future that are unavailable at the moment. Each generation marvels at how past ones put up with systems and notions later banished as cruel and ludicrous. History books are notoriously short on mercy and absolution. We must look to God, and to each other, for that.

American Conquest and Indigenous Peoples
What issues confronted these future American saints? What matters of the soul and society became their special missions by the simple juxtaposition of time and place?

Evangelization is always and everywhere the first great mission of Christianity. Heroes of the Church in each century seek to faithfully present the good news of Jesus Christ to the world. Still it should be noted: what Saint Paul did among his fellow Roman citizens—all Greek-speaking peoples of Asia Minor enjoying a homogenous culture and way of life—cannot be duplicated once the boundaries of a common context are crossed. It was hard enough to translate the very Jewish story of the Gospel to the gentile community; it would be another thing entirely to communicate Christianity to peoples who shared nearly none of the cultural markers of later evangelists.

In the context of the New World, the evangelistic effort was directed toward native communities who shared neither language nor worldview with the approaching missionaries. These missionaries from Spain and France had been sent out with the full backing of the Church to do the front work of colonizing for the throne. In fact, Church and throne were virtually one under the *patronato real* privilege granted by the pope to the Spanish monarchy. Essentially this gave Spain the right to appoint Church officials and craft its own missionary strategies.

In France, religion and state were likewise impossible to distinguish—although in that most anti-papal of nations, religious authority didn't come from Rome as a bequest but was simply assumed by the French government. Spanish friars and French Jesuits were sent to their respective American destinations, with the blessings of government, on the same mission: to "Christianize and civilize" the indigenous populations. They arrived only slightly in advance of conquistadors and businessmen who were coming, frankly, to get as rich as possible.

Compared with military personnel who were just as content to slaughter and eliminate, or enslave and exploit, native peoples, the priest-missionaries who corralled them into mission villages in the effort to save their souls have been described as being on the side of the angels in the New World conquest. However, the historical record draws few bright lines between the behavior of colonists and missionaries. Certainly there were disreputable characters on both sides. Some missionaries did strive to study the languages and cultures of the native peoples and to establish a dialogue of respect. The French had greater success in collaborating with the tribes in business dealings, and in making theological accommodations to native religious practices at the missions.

Spanish friars were the first to raise their voices when conquistadors and merchants mistreated these so-called Indians: "Are these not men? Have they not rational souls? Are you not bound to love them as you love yourselves?"[1] a Dominican friar said in accusation of his fellow colonialists as early as 1511. Tragically, the absence of a well-developed anthropology in the fifteenth century, combined with the missionaries' constricted idea of the terms of Christian salvation, plus the natives' utter lack of immunity to European diseases, spelled disaster for native communities, their way of life, and, in many cases, their outright survival.

Through recorded histories of the sixteenth-century Jesuit martyrs and Kateri Tekakwitha, we glimpse both sides of the trouble that results when such different worlds as France and native America collide, however benevolent the intent. If anything, the seventeenth- and eighteenth-century California missions of Friar Junípero Serra and those of the Spanish Southwest bore even more traumatic consequences for native peoples.

It has been argued that, colonialization being inevitable, the missions provided a temporary buffer of mediation between fatally clashing civilizations. The Church's engagement with indigenous communities wouldn't end with the ultimate failure of the missions, just as it didn't end for the American community at large. It was instead pushed forward into the future, to be visited again by nineteenth-century frontier saints like Mother Philippine Duchesne and Mother Theodore Guérin. Reconciling the damage of the past and healing the wound opened between the nation and its indigenous communities would become the lifelong work of Mother Katharine Drexel, well into the twentieth century.

Roman Catholics in a Protestant Land

Evangelization of native peoples was the primary goal of the Spanish and French missionaries in the New World. When the English threw their hats into the colonization ring, they had a different priority. From our secure American perspective in the twenty-first century, we Catholics might forget that this nation was not founded for our benefit. While the New World colonies of New France and New Spain were reflexively Catholic, most English settlers in the New World had, as a deliberate and articulated intent, the goal of gaining religious freedom *from* the Old World grasp of the popes, as well as powerful, state-sponsored churches of any kind. Historian Arthur Schlesinger, Sr., has called prejudice against Roman Catholicism in particular "the deepest bias in the history of the American people."[2] This bias would rear up in organized efforts to contain the feared influence of American Catholics, not only in the founding years of this society, but into the twentieth century.

The issue, simply stated, was this: How can a Roman Catholic possibly be an American? Doesn't the allegiance of the Catholic person fundamentally lie in the direction of a foreign realm and distant potentate? This argument, raised most recently during the 1960 election campaign of John F. Kennedy, has shown remarkable endurance in our foundationally Protestant culture. The default suspicion, and sometimes outright repression, of the Catholic presence in the colonies and young United States took a heavy toll on the American saints and informed their path to a great degree. We can hardly appreciate their stories without appreciating this cultural dilemma.

Elizabeth Seton, for example, began her life as a comfortably respectable Anglican in British New York society in the late 1700s. After the death of her beloved husband, the central crisis of Seton's adult life was whether or not she could bear to lose everything and everyone else she valued by making full communion with Rome. Today, her discernment might be resolved with a few months of catechesis in a good RCIA program! For Seton, it meant years of anguish, ostracization by family and friends, the loss of home and community, and economic deprivation for herself and her children if she chose to become a Catholic.

A half century later in Indiana, Mother Theodore Guérin's community would face vandalism and arson, denial of credit and refusal of loans, and the shunning of their schools as a result of religious bias. Nineteenth-century nativist movements like the "Know-Nothing" party, and its later offshoot, the American Protective Association, were purposely founded to halt the economic progress and political influence of Catholics in this country. The "Know-Nothing" brand came from their practice of responding, "I know nothing" to all questions about the organization. Its purpose was to foment fears that Catholic immigrants hostile to American values were overrunning the country. It claimed that the pope sponsored this overwhelming influx of immigrants. The spirit such organizations roused within the frontier towns caused endless heartache for Mothers Philippine and Theodore, and created tremendous obstacles for Bishop Neumann in the Northeast as well. Likewise, Father Damien faced libel and humiliation in his work among the suffering people of Molokai that was, for him, as bad as contracting leprosy. The murmurs against Damien were driven by resentment of the strong Catholic missionary presence in the islands as much as toward the man personally. In the story of colonial Hawaii, the indigenous community was unopposed to Damien's courageous ministry, while many of its Protestant governors were apoplectic that a Catholic was getting all the credit for dealing with an epidemic they were challenged to address personally. Happily, Mother Marianne Cope and her sisters fared better when they arrived to care for Damien's afflicted population. Because of the accident of Mother Marianne's beauty and her personal radiance, one of the most powerful men in island government was enchanted by her and gave the sisters relentless cooperation.

The Protestant-Catholic divide in United States history has had long-lasting repercussions, and the distaste was by no means one-sided. In Mother Frances Cabrini's voluminous correspondence during her missionary voyages, disapproval and distrust of Protestants and their motives surface as a regular theme. Cabrini's astonishment when she meets a gracious, likeable Protestant is always genuine—and followed by a fervent wish to save his or her soul.

As a fact of history, Protestantism is rooted in spirited opposition to Roman Catholicism, an arguably sympathetic position in light of clerical and papal abuses of the sixteenth century. Catholic persecution of "heretics" and "schismatics" since the time of the Reformation contributed heartily to the fear and aggression many Protestants bore toward the Catholic Church. The ingrained American stance against "popery" has by no means vanished from all corners of our society, just as a general dismissal of or superior attitude toward Protestants persists among some Catholics.

Gratifyingly, many Christians have embraced the ecumenical spirit of the last century and are invested in building bridges of communication and common cause. It would be eccentric to think of Catholics as a persecuted group today, when a 2013 Pew Research Center study indicates there are presently 75 million U.S. Catholics, or one in four Americans. While the wound of Christian disunity in the Body of Christ is far from closed, it is on the road to healing.

A Century of Immigration

Three enormous concerns fell into the lap of the Catholic Church in America in the eighteenth century: immigration, education, and the abolition of slavery. Each was different, none were avoidable, and each impacted the others in unanticipated ways. From 1820 to 1920, the Catholic population in the United States increased from 195,000 to a staggering 18 million. From a mere 124 parishes and 150 clergy, the numbers of churches multiplied to 16,000 and priests to 21,000. The numbers of religious sisters rose dramatically in that century as well, from fewer than 900 to well over 100,000.

These figures do not represent an incredible baby boom and subsequent rush of vocations. The immigrant influx into the United States was responsible for this tremendous growth. The global migration itself was due to economic realities in places like Ireland, Germany, Poland, Mexico, and later, Italy. Not all immigrants were Catholic, but numbers were sufficient to heighten anti-Catholic sentiments and overwhelm Church resources. The sheer numbers involved in this mass migration of peoples, coupled with problems of language and inevitable social displacement, saturated the attention of the American Catholic hierarchy for an entire century.

This great century of immigration would also propel religious women like Guérin and Duchesne to leave France in order to aid the struggling American Church. It would entice priests like Neumann from Bohemia and Seelos from Germany to lend their assistance. Cope's family would migrate to New York State from Germany during these years, bringing their soon-to-be-exceptional daughter in tow. And Cabrini, terrified of water, was persuaded to get on her first boat and cross the Atlantic to bring relief to Italians toward the end of the migration wave.

If the first missionaries came to the New World under the motto "Christianize and civilize," the bishops of the United States three centuries later found themselves embracing the imperative to "Americanize" the incoming deluge of immigrants. Americanization meant more than teaching English to the newcomers. It also implied a thorough embrace of American identity that many of these economic refugees resisted. The Germans wanted to retain their mother tongue, and the Polish would not relinquish lay control of their parishes, especially to non-Polish clergy.

Both Italians and Mexicans had long accommodated local religious practices, along with Catholic rituals, to achieve a syncretic faith that seemed like superstition and nonsense to their French bishops and Irish pastors in the U.S. Also, Italian and Mexican communities shared a cultivated history of distrust in regard to clergy. While both groups viewed themselves as Catholic, they didn't feel the need for compulsory parish involvement or frequent recourse to the sacraments.

In the meantime, the constant westward press of the country's boundaries created stretches of clerical wasteland where many frontier folk simply didn't see enough Catholic hierarchy or ministry to retain their religious identity. As coastal cities bulged with the newcomers, the prospect of mid-west farms tempted some to chance a move westward.

Mining opportunities and the new railroad construction jobs in the far west beckoned to others. For Catholics in leadership, the question became how to hold this burgeoning American Church together under such explosive circumstances.

The answer coalesced in a new imperative for the American apostolate: education. Schools would provide the means for both Americanizing the children of immigrants and catechizing their parents.

The Birth of Catholic Schools
The idea of a Catholic school system wasn't new to the immigrant era. The first bishop of the new United States, John Carroll of Baltimore, regarded the establishment of a Catholic system of education in this country as an absolute priority. Carroll understood that, for Catholics to participate in U.S. society as equals, and to influence this society's moral development through a dialogue with political leadership, it would be necessary to develop a respectable American intellectual tradition. At the least, this implied not continuing to send their children to study abroad and not borrowing from European thought. Bishop Carroll established his first school, a seminary in Baltimore, in 1791—almost as soon as he received his appointment. Two colleges were soon to follow. Of course, homegrown priests would not be immediately forthcoming, so clergy and bishops continued to be imported, mostly from France and Ireland.

The first U.S.-born priests had hardly begun to take their places in parishes when the staggering waves of immigrants began to arrive; this meant that foreign-born clergy were still required in large numbers to assist the See of Baltimore through the crisis. The continually overburdened clergy could not undertake wide-scale religious instruction in the midst of such demand. Women religious were needed to embrace the challenge.

Even while Bishop Carroll scoured Europe for sufficient numbers of these women, he also discovered one right in his parochial backyard: the new convert Elizabeth Seton. Duchesne, Guérin, and Cabrini also joined the ranks of women who built the Catholic school system in the

United States on their backs and up until their final breaths. It must be noted that tens of thousands of women religious were involved in this heroic work, many of whose names will never be lifted up through canonization. In addition, these women brought the advantages of literacy and religious education to adults on the frontiers. In many cases they brought an end to prejudice among their Protestant neighbors, who marveled at their sterling examples and brought their own children to the schools.

A common school system in the United States—what we now know as public schools—did not spring up at once after the Revolutionary War. In parts of the U.S. the Catholic school, once opened, became the *only* school available, and local governments funded some as a result. What common schools did exist in the early 1800s, prior to this Catholic school initiative, were mainly to be found in urban areas. They were also unmistakably Protestant, which often implied an anti-Catholic bias tucked into the agenda. Since colonial times, school prayer and Bible-reading had been standard parts of the curriculum, both taught from a Protestant perspective and over the objections of Catholic parents. Little could be done to change this, as colonial Catholics were legally disallowed in many states from opening their own schools, just as they were often forbidden to build churches, to vote without taking offensive oaths against their beliefs, and to attend Mass except in private homes.

Once the new nation was established, however, Catholics could and did worship publicly, and proceeded to create an alternative school system. Pastors and their communities set to work doing both—but not necessarily in that order. Some Catholic communities, especially among the German-born, built the church first and *then* petitioned the bishop for a priest to provide services. In other places, the school rose before the church, which some bishops encouraged. Archbishop John Hughes of New York was not alone in insisting to his priests: "Build the school-house first, and the church afterwards."[3] Many among the hierarchy were convinced that if the Catholic community had no understanding of its faith, providing a sacramental ministry was useless.

In the 1850s and 1860s, some U.S. bishops ordered every pastor in their dioceses to build a parochial school under pain of mortal sin, and denied communion to parents who proved willing to throw their children to the wolves by sending them to the common schools. Although it became official policy at the Third Plenary Council of Baltimore in 1884 to make a school practically mandatory in every Catholic parish, in reality, compliance was never forthcoming, mostly due to lack of funds and personnel. Philadelphia Bishop John Neumann, however, took the mandate to heart, and created the first diocesan school system in the country.

Abolition and the Negro Question
Msgr. John Tracy Ellis, celebrated as the dean of American church historians in the twentieth century, was often brutally honest about the shortcomings of the Church and its unwillingness to own up to the more troubling passages of its history. Regarding the practice of slavery in America, Ellis describes the prevalent views of the leading theologian of the nineteenth century, Bishop Francis Patrick Kenrick, in unflinching terms:

> Official Catholic doctrine held that slavery was not necessarily evil; it taught that slavery, thought of theoretically and apart from specific abuses to human dignity, was not opposed to the divine or natural law. Manumission was encouraged wherever circumstances would permit the slave to better his condition, and strong emphasis was always placed on the moral obligation of Catholic slave owners to treat their subjects with justice and charity and to see that they received religious instruction. Moreover, the Church's condemnation of the slave trade was definite.[4]

Twenty-first-century readers might find it chilling to imagine that any ethical person, much less a prominent theologian, might ever contemplate slavery "theoretically and apart from specific abuses to human dignity." What is perhaps worse for us today is to consider Kenrick's conclusion in regard to the abolitionist cause: "Nevertheless, since such is the state of things, nothing should be attempted against the laws nor anything be done or said that would make them bear their yoke unwillingly."[5]

In a theological climate such as this, it's not surprising to find Mother Theodore Guérin writing in her journal:

> The most painful sight I saw in New Orleans was the selling of slaves. Every day in the streets at appointed places, negroes and negresses in holiday attire are exposed for this shameful traffic. This spectacle oppressed my heart.... I would have wished to buy them all that I might say to them, "Go! Bless Providence. You are free!"[6]

The record of the American church in the mid-eighteenth century was not uniform on the issue of slavery. Voices were raised on both sides of the question, but there was no official consensus. Bishop John Carroll's family owned slaves, as did Carroll, to the day of his death. Jesuits were slave owners who financed their rural ministries with plantations in the South. Mother Philippine deplored the practice and yet her Sacred Heart Sisters made peace with it, to the point of accepting slaves when supplied in certain settings. Predictably, most Southern bishops were against abolition; many Northern ones spoke out in favor of it, though not all. When the Civil War broke out, more than forty priests served as chaplains on the Union side, and about thirty did the same with the Confederate armies. Eight hundred sisters also served as nurses in makeshift hospitals on both sides of the conflict.

After the war, however, the hierarchy in the United States spoke with one voice. At the Second Plenary Council of Baltimore in 1866, it was decreed that assisting the Negro community with schools and religious instruction had a high priority. This was the same century that viewed schools as the best answer to the immigrant question. With education came integration into society and enhanced opportunity. Given this parallel tactic, the results of the Council were the closest thing to equal treatment that the newly freed Negro population might expect.

The plan to hasten the assimilation of the black community into the American story by means of education and catechesis was well meant, but badly misjudged. Sometimes the will to serve blacks was lacking in the local white church. Even where resolve was strong, there was often no money in the war-impoverished Church of the South or the already painfully stretched immigrant North. Even when both will and funds were available, schools were opened only to be burned by those who did not approve of the effort.

The mission to educate and improve the lot of the Negro community would be left to the very few black Catholic congregations, or to white religious orders, assigned by local bishops to serve the black community, who were then thrown upon their own resources to survive. It was into this divisive and sometimes dangerous moral predicament that Katharine Drexel, a shy and sheltered white Philadelphia heiress, would find herself inexplicably thrust as the nation moved into the twentieth century. She would spearhead renewed efforts on the part of American Catholics to keep their promises to both the Native American and the African American communities at a time when both were near to forsaken by the larger Church.

The Healing Ministries
It would be impossible to talk about Christianity without acknowledging its mandate to promote the healing ministry of Jesus. From the time of the apostles, some saints have been endowed with the miraculous ability to heal. In fact, the canonization process has always held verifiable healing miracles as among the most recognizable signs of a holy person—whether they are performed during the saint's life, or occur after his or her death in response to intercession.

The "wow" factor of miraculous healings can sometimes distract us from seeing that the healing ministry of the Church encompasses much more than a scattering of miracles throughout history. It also involves the willingness to defend the sick publicly in policy and decision-making; to comfort them with presence and visitation; to soothe them with touch and medicines; and to acknowledge the dignity and humanity of all who are ill, disabled, and dying.

Because of the crystal clarity of this Gospel summons, the Church has always been in the health care business. Our U.S. saints are no exception. Mother Cabrini originally arrived in the Americas as an evangelist and educator. She quickly realized that establishing a health care network across the United States was to be a considerable and integral part of that vocation. While Mother Theodore Guérin is viewed primarily as an educator, she also opened pharmacies in Indiana and was well versed in the use of local herbs and natural medicines. Philippine Duchesne took care of the sick before and after she came to America, sometimes as the official infirmarian of her community and sometimes simply because everyone else was sick. Katharine Drexel's community viewed care of the sick as part of their overall ministry among indigenous and black communities.

Father Francis Xavier Seelos certainly saw himself as a typical parish priest during most of his U.S. assignments. But when the yellow fever epidemic drove most able-bodied people out of New Orleans, Seelos stayed to minister to the sick and dying until he succumbed to the fever himself. Likewise, Father Damien came to the islands of the Pacific to pastor indigenous peoples through a traditional sacramental ministry. However, he spent the most significant years of his life, and gave himself up to death, ministering among those afflicted with leprosy in the segregated colony at Molokai, a community the world was loath to approach.

Mother Marianne Cope, by contrast, began her ministry in hospitals, consciously intending to pursue a vocation in health care. It was that passion to ease the suffering of the sick that compelled her to leave a comfortable administrative position in upstate New York hospitals to devote herself hands-on to the feared leprosy sufferers in Hawaii.

Many U.S. saints were no strangers to ill health themselves, but endured chronic illnesses that plagued them across their lifetimes. Kateri Tekakwitha was a smallpox survivor who lost her family to an epidemic. She carried the disfiguring scars of that illness until her death. Junípero Serra walked the length of California on a damaged, swollen leg. Elizabeth Seton contracted the tuberculosis that brought her husband's life to an early end and periodically limited her exertions.

Mother Cabrini was considered so physically frail she was hardly expected to survive her first voyage across the Atlantic. She suffered from recurring bouts of fever, probably due to early malaria exposure that weakened her lungs and heart. Mother Guérin endured a digestive ailment caused by smallpox and suffered from lifelong pleurisy that confined her to bed for weeks every winter. Philippine Duchesne, another smallpox survivor, also endured scurvy on shipboard, yellow fever in New Orleans, and in Missouri she contracted erysipelas, a streptococcus bacterial scourge that intermittently caused swelling in her limbs for the rest of her life.

Damien and Seelos both contracted and died from the diseases that were the crux of their respective ministries. Neither Mother Marianne Cope nor her sisters ever caught the disease to which they were daily exposed, but Cope did struggle with heart and kidney failure in her final years, brought on by the endlessly long days and deprivations of her ministry. Katharine Drexel suffered from a heart condition in the last four decades of her life and was bedridden for years. The Jesuit martyrs Jogues, Goupil, and Lalande shared in a unique way the anguish of the world in the final surrender of their bodies to their persecutors.

The "wounded healer" isn't a contradiction in the realm of faith, but actually a familiar paradigm. Despite the Easter victory, the resurrected Christ still bears the wounds of the cross in his glorified body. Where suffering persists in the world, despite the personal cost, the Christian mandate is to remain and to serve.

The Legacy of American Saints

Across the lives of these women and men, recognized for their labors in this country, we can read the story of our nation. We can also gain insight and wisdom for our own times, because their questions have not ceased to be relevant. How does the Church in the present century fulfill its summons to evangelize those who have not heard the good news of Jesus? Is it possible to be a good Catholic and a good American today, and how do we offer our truest allegiance to both identities? What is happening in the ecumenical movement now, and have we advanced the original American goal—genuine freedom of religion—to include all faiths represented in our population?

How do we respond to the new immigrant presence today, and how best can the Church serve them and include them in the American story? What role should Catholic schools and institutes of higher learning now assume, and how does the Catholic intellectual tradition influence critical issues of our generation? What part does the U.S. church play in the racial issues of our times, and what might we do to promote healing of the old wounds of centuries past? What are the present challenges to the health of the body of Christ, and how do we remain with and serve those who are injured, ill, and dying today?

The women and men whose lives are the primary subjects of this book have given us their answers. They have written them in years and sacrifices, sometimes in love and tenderness, sometimes in steely faith and firm resolve, often in courageous actions, and even in blood. As we read these stories, we're astounded by the responses these very human beings gave to circumstances we can scarcely imagine facing ourselves. What would we have done? Given the issues facing this generation of American Catholics, what will we do now? If these holy lives invite us to address such questions, their canonization has achieved its purpose.

Part Two

Biographies of the American Saints

1] **Isaac Jogues** (1607–1646), **René Goupil** (1608–1642), and **Jean de Lalande** (d. 1646)
Missionary Heroes of the New World
Feast: October 19. Beatified: 1925. Canonized: 1930.

It must be that my body suffer the fire of earth, in order to deliver those poor souls from the flames of Hell; it must die a transient death, in order to procure for them an eternal life.[1]

It was a noble and heroic mission upon which these good men embarked in the seventeenth century. Just decades earlier, in 1540, Spanish knight Ignatius of Loyola and his college friends Francis Xavier and Peter Faber had founded the Society of Jesus, a religious order of men who would be soldiers of God. These spiritual marines served in the trenches of evangelization: teaching, preaching, and celebrating the sacraments for the sake of saving souls. When the going got tough, the Jesuits would get going.

Pope Paul VI famously said of this indomitable Society:

> Wherever in the Church, even in the most difficult and extreme field, in the crossroads of ideologies, in the front line of social conflict, there has been and there is confrontation between the deepest desires of the human person and the perennial message of the Gospel, there too, there have been, and there are, Jesuits.[2]

There was no tougher theater of missionary work than the New World. At the same time, there was no greater chance for missionary glory than among the indigenous people—bereft of European culture and Christian religion—that colonialists were finding all over the North American continent.

Spanish Franciscans were working the southern settlements of New Spain, from the Florida peninsula to the gulf shores of Texas and beyond to California. English Protestants were spreading out in New England and along the Atlantic seaboard. New France—the land stretching from Acadia west across upstate New York, fording the St. Lawrence into Canada, onward to the Great Lakes, and down the Mississippi to the Gulf of Mexico—was the territory of the Huron, the Algonquin, and the Iroquois, possessors of the land before any written history. This would be the arena of the great Jesuit enterprise.

But what brought France to the New World in the first place? The answer is simple: money. And that money was to be made in the lucrative fur trade. Prior to the seventeenth century, the indigenous peoples of North America had traded pelts among themselves for generations. But with the arrival of the Europeans, the opportunities for economic gain greatly expanded. Everybody wanted to get into the act.

With the establishment of Quebec City on the north banks of the St. Lawrence River in 1608, French explorer and cartographer Samuel de Champlain initiated the startup. Bankrolled by the king of France, Champlain was expected to turn a profit from his explorations. When he started sending back boatloads of fur—pelts of the beaver, sea otter, deer, bear, ermine, and even the lowly skunk—the market took off. Beaver pelts especially attracted European haberdashers; they made for excellent hats, and the fashion became the rage. From that point on, no beaver in New France was safe.

To build the enterprise, Champlain established relations with locals who knew where the beaver were and how to get them. They were the Iroquois of the Five Nations: the Mohawk, Oneida, Onondaga, Cayuga, and Seneca. They lived at along the St. Lawrence River, in northern New York, and around the Great Lakes. Other players on the supply side were the Algonquin, known to any New Englander by their local names: the Wampanoag, Massachusett, Nipmuck, Passamaquoddy, Quinnipiac, Mohegan, Pequot, Tunxis, and Narragansett. They were found in eastern Quebec and New England and made their living by hunting, fishing, and the fur trade.

Exploring west to the Great Lakes, Champlain made contact with the Wendat, better known as the Huron, near Georgian Bay, and made a deal with them for their beaver skins in exchange for military support against their enemy, the Mohawk to the south.

During the summer of 1609, Champlain drove south from the St. Lawrence with a small company of French soldiers and some three hundred Huron, mapping river valleys to the vast lake that would later bear his name. There, near present-day Ticonderoga, he encountered a force of several hundred Mohawk and the battle was on. Possessing superior firepower, the French-Huron alliance routed the Mohawk; Champlain himself, by his own account, dropped two Mohawk chiefs with one shot. This fight established hostilities between the Mohawk and the French for the next hundred years.

Thus the seventeenth-century battle lines were drawn in New France. The Huron allied with the French and supplied French traders with furs in exchange for military support, weapons, and European dry goods. The Mohawk threw in their lot and their pelts with the Dutch, who were moving up the Hudson Valley from Manhattan.

With the European technology of iron axes, knives, fishhooks, and guns introduced into the hunt, the beaver population of the St. Lawrence became seriously over-harvested, escalating the violence between the French-Huron alliance and the Mohawk-Dutch coalition over control of expanding trapping grounds. Nevertheless the French fur trade, French merchants, and more importantly the French Crown, enjoyed huge economic success, drawing additional ships, manpower, and capital investment into New France.

It was to this enterprise that the Jesuits hitched their wagon. The New World was a wonderful opportunity for these missionaries to do what they were trained to do, inspired to do, and called by God to do. The Good Lord had said in the Bible to preach the Gospel to *all the nations*—and that those who believed and were baptized would be saved, while those who didn't would be damned. The French Jesuits now had the opportunity, as well as the mandate, to save souls. And save souls they would, even at the cost of their own lives.

Father Jean de Brébeuf was the first Jesuit missionary to the people of New France. Brébeuf had mastered the Huron language during a three-year stay at Wendake, the heart of the Huron nation on Georgian Bay. His exploits among the Huron were being published in *The Jesuit Relations*, a chronicle of missionary activity that began appearing in France in 1632.

In 1633, Brébeuf returned to Wendake for a second hitch, but his mission quickly ran aground. A smallpox epidemic in 1634, followed by a season of malignant influenza in 1636 and smallpox again in 1639, slaughtered the Huron in massive numbers. Their population, estimated by Champlain to be originally in the area of 30,000, was reduced to a mere 12,000. The Huron blamed it on Brébeuf with his strange teachings, strange ceremonies, and the strange signs he made over dying people. The priest was beaten, his many crosses in the villages destroyed, and his chapel damaged. To make matters worse, Brébeuf fell on the ice, broke his shoulder, and was obliged to return to Quebec.

During this time the Huron were suffering increasing attacks by the Mohawk, who were determined to grab the rich trapping land of the Huron. Backed by the Dutch, who were anxious to see the French fur trade in Dutch hands, the well-armed Mohawk enjoyed a military advantage.

Much like boys anywhere, who grow up idolizing sports heroes, Isaac Jogues, the fifth of nine children born to a middle-class family in Orléans, France, was enthralled as a youth reading the exploits of Brébeuf in *The Jesuit Relations*. After his study at the Jesuit college in Orléans, Jogues entered the novitiate at Rouen where he encountered Louis Lallemant, an inspiring teacher who instilled in him a passion for the missionary life. Continuing his studies at Collège de Clermont in Paris, Jogues distinguished himself with a thorough knowledge of Greek and Latin, eloquent oratory, and a refined comportment. Anxious for the missions, he concluded his studies and was ordained in 1636.

In April of that same year he embarked for New France, an eight-week journey across the Atlantic, followed by stops at several outposts along the St. Lawrence, and finally on to Quebec and Trois-Rivières. There he met up with some Jesuits returning from the missions, emaciated and spent, broken and scarred from their work. Rather than frightening off the young priest, his ruined confreres greatly encouraged him.

What Jogues had learned from his studies and experienced in his life of devotion was the mystical truth of what Jesus called "the kingdom of God." In this kingdom Jesus taught that the last would be first, the lowly would be lifted up, the persecuted and reviled would rejoice, and the dead would rise. Jogues had no misgivings whatsoever about surrendering himself to suffering, and even death, in the missions. For him, the heavenly reward was far too great to pass up.

Apart from the obvious lack of creature comforts in New France—impossibly cold winters, lack of supplies, the constant threat of disease and famine—the young missionary faced a far more difficult challenge: the clash of European and Indian cultures.

After sixteen more days of arduous journey by river and overland portage, Jogues arrived in Wendake in September, at the mission of Sainte-Marie among the Hurons, near present-day Midland, Ontario, on Georgian Bay. The elegant, urbane Frenchman must have shown remarkable courage and endurance during the long journey because the Huron started calling him *Ondessonk*, a word that has been variously translated as "the indomitable one," or "the raptor."

It was at the mission Sainte-Marie that Jogues joined up with his hero, Jean de Brébeuf.

Shortly after his arrival, Jogues took sick with fever. He survived, but the ensuing epidemic among the Huron became so grave that in 1637 the Huron governing council passed a resolution that all the Jesuit missionaries must die. The immune system of the Huron—in fact of all the indigenous people of North America—was unprepared to defend against viruses that the Europeans, whether soldier, trapper, trader, or missionary, brought to the New World.

Thankfully the Huron decree was not carried out. The Huron, unlike their enemy the Mohawk, were not a particularly violent people. They would fight, but usually in defense. They weren't given to military sorties; they preferred a peaceful home life. This made them attractive to the missionaries and particularly receptive to the Christian Gospel of peace. They got along fairly well with the Jesuits.

Still, the Huron culture couldn't possibly assimilate everything that came with the Jesuits. There was the language problem. Brébeuf had warned the missionaries that it was pointless to try to teach the Huron to speak French. Why should they learn? It was up to the Jesuits to learn the Huron language and thereby communicate. But the Huron language had no words for such subtle Christian concepts as God, heaven, hell, eternity, Trinity, sin, salvation, conscience, and the like.

The Huron had a lot of trouble understanding why a Supreme Being would punish someone or condemn a person to everlasting torture in a place called hell. Nor could they fathom how pouring water on a person's head could change that person's status from hell-bent to heaven-bound. They understood magic, but transubstantiation didn't produce the verifiable evidence they needed to accept the doctrine.

Other practices left some of the Huron suspicious of the Jesuits' intent. The missionaries were always looking for gravely ill people, especially children and babies who were near death. They would dutifully perform the sacraments of the dying for them, ensuring their passage into heaven. But the Huron only saw the link between the ceremony and the resulting death of the person.

The seemingly magic sign of the four-point cross, the mysterious oil, and the indecipherable incantation, always in Latin, could not help but suggest a cause and effect relationship to the Huron. And while the Huron often died of the fever, the Jesuits managed to survive. How? Some thought the answer was in the secret drink contained in the jeweled chalice from which only the priest drank. No one else was ever allowed to drink from, or even touch, the enchanted cup.

It was not that the Huron were irreligious. They had their beliefs in the supernatural, their ceremonies, their mysteries. They were just not the same as those of the French Christians. No more than a Catholic in France might accept the religious beliefs of the Huron, would a Huron accept the beliefs of the French Catholic. But the Huron were an intellectually curious people and they kept the Jesuits around. They liked the quiet, gentle demeanor of the missionaries, and the fervor of their preaching. In times of hunger and deprivation, they didn't mind the material resources of the French, either. It was reported in *The Jesuit Relations* that the Huron would delight in asking the missionaries questions and then erupt in uproarious laughter at the attempts by the priests to answer in the Huron tongue.

Another practice of the Jesuits, curious to the Huron—and, indeed, to all indigenous groups—was their long hours spent writing. The Jesuits' European superiors required the missionaries to send home detailed reports of their activities, which would keep headquarters informed and, at the same time, be useful in drumming up support for the missionary enterprise. The reports, heavily edited by Jesuit officials, would appear in *The Jesuit Relations*, giving readers romantic accounts of the missionaries' exploits among the "noble savages" of New France.

The Huron, having never developed or even seen a written language, were mystified by the scribbling. For some, the strange marks that flowed from the missionaries' pens left them more suspicious than ever of the Jesuits. Conspiracy theories arose; perhaps the letters spelled out diabolical formulae that brought down disease upon their loved ones.

Despite all these challenges, Jogues and his companions pressed on with their mission of saving souls. They were, after all, priests imbued with the power to wash the stain of sin from the souls of the people whom they encountered, among whom they lived, and with whom they truly fell in love over the course of their years in New France. Though the script they were given was unlikely to produce the desired results, follow it they did, whole-heartedly, faithfully, and heroically, to the loss of their health and welfare, even to the shedding of their blood.

Meanwhile, back in France, other young men yearned for the adventure of the missions. In March of 1639, René Goupil, an academically trained practitioner of the developing art of medical surgery, inspired by the reports in *The Jesuit Relations*, left his practice and entered the Jesuit novitiate. Unable to complete his studies due to a hearing impairment, Goupil nonetheless headed for New France and, in 1640, at a Jesuit mission near Quebec City, presented himself and his surgical skills for service as a *donné*, a "given man," to the Jesuits.

Donnés were remarkable men. For one reason or another they were not incorporated into the Society of Jesus by the customary religious vows, but they were connected to the Jesuits by an agreement, sometimes written and notarized, by which the *donné* placed himself squarely into the hands of the Jesuits, completely at their disposal to do with as they wished, and who in turn guaranteed that the *donné* would be housed, fed, and cared for in case of illness, for the rest of his life or until the expiration of the contract.

In June of 1642, Isaac Jogues was sent from Sainte-Marie to Quebec City to bring a sick missionary to the hospital and to pick up supplies. Returning via Trois-Rivières, the *donné* Goupil was added to the manifest, along with a few more Frenchmen and a large company of Huron Christian neophytes and catechumens.

On the second day of their journey back to Sainte-Marie, the twelve-canoe convoy was ambushed by a contingent of Mohawk pirates who were keeping the St. Lawrence under surveillance. After a brief firefight from which most of the French and Huron fled, Goupil, another Frenchman, and several Huron were taken captive. Jogues, watching from concealment in the bushes, later wrote that he couldn't bear to leave his companions. He was the only priest among them, and for them to die without the ministry of a priest was unthinkable to Jogues. He revealed himself and surrendered to the Mohawk.

Jogues, Goupil and the others were force-marched some 270 miles from the St. Lawrence to the Mohawk central compound, Ossernenon, now Auriesville, on the Mohawk River in upstate New York. There the prisoners were forced to run the gauntlet, a practice by which captives were made to pass between two rows of men, women, and children with sticks, who would beat the gauntleteers with great energy.

While this practice understandably seemed cruel to the Europeans, it reflected a concept in both Mohawk and Huron culture by which captives were incorporated, and essentially initiated, into the community. Enemy prisoners were taken as a way of replacing those who had been killed by the enemy. The gauntlet was used to "beat out" the captives' old identity. After the initiation they were assimilated into village life, treated fairly well by their captors, and given relatively free range.

Not that there wasn't cruel treatment from the nastier factions of the society. The Mohawk knew magic, and they knew how to turn their enemy's magic against them. It seemed to many Mohawk that the secret to Jesuit survival was in the jewel-encrusted gold cups from which the priests, and only the priests, drank a liquid they called the "Blood of Christ." The Mohawk were forbidden to even touch it. Familiar with the cult of Jesuit priests, they knew that the three "canonical fingers" of the priest—the thumb, index, and middle fingers with which the priest held the sacred host and chalice—were essential in the celebration of the Mass. During Isaac Jogues's torture, they cut off—some say chewed off—the fingers, thereby rendering him incapable of performing the suspect ceremony. Some years later, in 1649, the Iroquois would "baptize" Jogues's mentor, Jean de Brébeuf, with boiling water.

With their identity beaten out of them (or, in Jogues's case, cut off), Jogues and Goupil settled into village life. In keeping with their vocation, they maintained "church" with the captive Huron Christians and even attempted to catechize the Mohawk. But both saw the handwriting on the wall: in all likelihood neither would survive. Goupil asked for and was granted entry into the Jesuit order from Jogues, who received his vows. A few days later, on September 29, 1642, Goupil was hacked to death by an enraged Mohawk who had caught him making the Sign of the Cross over his daughter. Thus René Goupil became the first Jesuit martyr of North America.

Jogues remained in Ossernenon another year. Then, in November of 1643, with the help of Dutch fur traders, he escaped the Mohawk and made his way to the Dutch settlement of New Amsterdam, thus becoming the first Catholic priest to set foot on Manhattan Island. From there he sailed to France where it took some time for his Jesuit superiors to believe it was really he.

While in France, Jogues requested and received an indult from Pope Urban VIII to celebrate Mass without the missing canonical fingers.

Rested and recovered from his ordeal, Jogues wasted no time returning to the land he loved and the mission to which he was called. He arrived back in Quebec in 1644, but was kept from outlying missions because of the dicey situation with the Mohawk. Eventually the Mohawk ambassador Kiotseaeton worked out a deal for an exchange of prisoners with the Canadian Governor Montmagny and subsequently, in 1646, a peace treaty was put in place.

The governor hoped to wrest the fur trade from the Dutch by persuading the Mohawk to switch allegiances. The Jesuits were eager to get back into the mission game. Both agreed to send Isaac Jogues to his former captors as peace ambassador. To this appointment, Jogues reacted with great joy and fearful dread. "Poor nature," he wrote to his superior, "which remembered the past, trembled; but.... Could I endure that it should depend on me that some soul were not saved?"[3] Happy to plunge into the field once more, Jogues left Quebec for Mohawk country in May of 1646.

Now a priest-diplomat, Jogues found the fearful Mohawk somewhat inclined to peaceful relations with the French. The talks went well and Jogues returned to Quebec City two months later with a favorable report. In September, Jogues was back among the Mohawk, this time with a contingent of Huron who wanted to protect their financial interests in any trade deal with the Mohawk. Jogues was accompanied by a young *donné*, Jean de Lalande, who'd spent time with him at Sante-Marie.

The Mohawk were not happy about the Huron presence in the diplomatic entourage. Nor had they been particularly pleased with the epidemic, drought, and crop failure that followed Jogues's spring visit, all of which they blamed on the Jesuit. Within weeks, Isaac Jogues and Jean de Lalande were placed under arrest and put on trial at Ossernenon, the place Jogues feared most. The moderate majority of the Mohawk were satisfied to let them off with a warning, but the more hawkish authorities would have none of it. On October 18, 1646, Isaac Jogues and Jean de Lalande were attacked and killed by an assassin and their bodies thrown into the Mohawk River. They joined their fellow missionary, René Goupil, in becoming the first sainted martyrs of the future United States.

Ironically and prophetically, from the very same clay upon which these amazing men shed their blood, a new hope for America was formed. Just ten years after the Mohawk of Ossernenon witnessed the violent deaths of Jogues and Lalande, they celebrated the sweet birth of a girl child, daughter of a Mohawk chief and his Algonquin wife. They named her Ioragode, which means Little Sunshine. She would grow up to become Kateri Tekakwitha, the Lily of the Mohawks, the first Native American to be declared a saint.

Today

Eight men died in the missions of New France and were celebrated as saints on both sides of the border between the U.S. and Canada: René Goupil (1642), Isaac Jogues (1646), Jean de Lalande (1646), Antoine Daniel (1648), Jean de Brébeuf (1649), Noël Chabanel (1649), Charles Garnier (1649), and Gabriel Lalemant (1649). The National Shrine to the North American Martyrs was created at the site of their deaths in Auriesville, New York. The Huron were greatly reduced by disease and war in the seventeenth century. Huron remain in Quebec, Oklahoma, Michigan, and Kansas. Mohawk peoples still live in northern New York, along the St. Lawrence, and in southern Ontario.

Timeline

1607: Isaac Jogues born in Orléans, France
1615: Explorer Samuel de Champlain encounters the Huron at Georgian Bay
1620: The Mayflower lands at Plymouth
1624: Tobacco gains popularity; Pope Urban VIII threatens users with excommunication
1626: The Dutch purchase Manhattan Island from the Wappinger for $24 worth of fish hooks and trinkets
1630: Disease kills two-thirds of Huron population
1633: Galileo brought before the Inquisition
1636: Jogues arrives at Sainte-Marie
1642: Jogues and René Goupil arrested by the Mohawk; Goupil killed at Ossernenon
1643: Jogues escapes to France
1646: Jogues returns to Ossernenon with Jean de Lalande; both killed October 18

21] Kateri Tekakwitha
(1656–1680)
The Lily of the Mohawks
Feast: July 14 (U.S.), April 17 (Canada). Venerable: 1943.
Beatified: 1980. Canonized: 2012.

I am not my own; I have given myself to Jesus. He must be my only love.[1]

In this world there are holy places and graced moments. They occur when eternity breaks into time, when heaven itself comes to earth. At the Church of the Holy Sepulcher in Jerusalem, a stone is preserved upon which the body of the crucified Christ, it is believed, was laid to rest. It is a magnet for pilgrims seeking to connect with the grace of God. The devout bring their rosaries to touch to the stone. Mothers bring T-shirts purchased in the gift shop for their children, hoping to soak up the grace present in the rock. This holy place still echoes the graced moment in history when time stood still and heaven emerged from the depths of the earth.

Far from Jerusalem, on the other side of the world, another place was made holy by death and the renewal of life. It is in Auriesville, New York, forty miles northwest of Albany. It too is a shrine where pilgrims go to connect with grace. As mentioned in our last chapter, Auriesville is the site of Ossernenon, the seventeenth-century Mohawk village where, by 1646, three of the Jesuit martyrs of North America—Isaac Jogues, René Goupil, and Jean de Lalande—had met their deaths.

In that very same holy place, only ten years later, a girl child was born who would also become a saint. They called her Ioragode, a Mohawk name meaning Little Sunshine. Her parents had what we might call a mixed marriage. Her father, Kenneronkwa, was a chief among the Mohawk. Her mother, Tagaskouita, was a captive Algonquin.

The Mohawk were indigenous people of North America living in what today is upstate New York, along the Mohawk and Hudson Rivers. They ranged eastward to the mountains of New England, northward to the St. Lawrence River, westward to the Finger Lakes, and southward along the Hudson to the present northern border of New Jersey. They were the easternmost nation of the Iroquois Confederacy. This powerful coalition would play a pivotal role in the European colonization of North America, and would continue to influence American history through the Revolutionary War period.

The name Mohawk comes from the Dutch rendering of a Mohican name that means "people who live with the bears." Bears were plentiful in upstate New York. The Mohawk first gained their wealth and political power from trade in the flint market, a resource abundant in their territory and used in toolmaking and weapons manufacture. After contact with Dutch fur traders coming up the Hudson, the Mohawk also cornered the lucrative market in beaver pelts by driving their Algonquin competitors out of the northern trapping grounds.

It was during this conflict over trapping grounds that the Mohawk commander Kenneronkwa met Tagaskouita, an Algonquin captive. The war-practice of the Mohawk, and indeed all Iroquois and Algonquin, was to take captives. Over time, the captives were indoctrinated and incorporated into the community. Captives were understood to be replacing those killed or captured by the enemy in raids and skirmishes. Consequently, it was common to find Algonquin living among the Mohawk, and Mohawk among the Algonquin.

If God meant for opposites to attract, then the romance between Kenneronkwa and Tagaskouita was a match made in heaven. Kenneronkwa was a fighter and embraced the animistic religious faith common to the Mohawk. He believed all things possessed a living spirit and that these spirits influenced, and even controlled, the progression of events in this world. He participated in Mohawk festivals of the seasons, and the agricultural and hunting calendar.

Tagaskouita, on the other hand, had been raised among Jesuit missionaries in the New France colony of Trois-Rivières along the St. Lawrence River between Quebec City and Montreal. Here she learned the Catholic religion and had been baptized. Her capture by the Mohawk cut short her religious development. While Christianity was not unknown among the Mohawk, they were suspicious of the religion—and for good reason.

The missionaries known to the Mohawk were French; the French were allied with the Huron, competitors in the all-important fur trade. And, they were trying to Europeanize the people. The religion of the Jesuit was strange, seemingly conducted in a language neither French nor Iroquois. The Mohawk were a free and noble people and were not comfortable with all the inscrutable rules and regulations of French culture and religion.

Finally, and most importantly, the French arrived in their territory carrying deadly pathogens that overwhelmed the native immune system. Smallpox and yellow fever wiped out thousands of Mohawk. Moreover, the Jesuits rarely contracted the disease, and if they did, they recovered, while the Mohawk died in droves.

It was to this Mohawk world that Tagaskouita was brought after her capture. And it was in this context that she met and married Kenneronkwa. Marriage among the Mohawk was an honored institution and a lifelong commitment. In Mohawk culture, the wife was head of the household. All wealth and property were under her control. Mohawk women enjoyed great esteem.

Soon, in 1656, Tagaskouita gave birth to Little Sunshine. But when she was four years old, a smallpox epidemic swept through the village of Ossernenon. Many died, including Little Sunshine's parents and a brother. The girl also contracted the illness.

Smallpox is an infectious disease caused by an airborne virus. The virus invades multiple organs in the human body, most notably the mouth, throat, skin, and internal organs. Among Native Americans in the seventeenth century, the disease was fatal in eighty to ninety percent of the cases. Little Sunshine survived her bout with smallpox and was taken in by her father's sister. But the disease left her face scarred by the distinguishing skin lesions. It also left her eyesight impaired by corneal ulcerations. Soon after her recovery, the active four-year-old, now learning to live with poor vision, received a new name: Tekakwitha, or "she who bumps into things."

With disease and increased competition in the fur trade, the strength of the Mohawk began to fade. In 1666, a French military force attacked Ossernenon, drove the people from the village, and burned it to the ground. Winter was fast approaching. The crops were gone and the community lacked adequate shelter. The Mohawk were forced to capitulate. They entered into a peace treaty with the French, agreeing, among other things, to allow Jesuit missionaries to live among them and teach their children. After the Mohawk compound, now called Caughnawaga, was rebuilt on the other side of the Mohawk River, Jesuit Father Jean Pierron and two other priests arrived to run the mission.

This presented a real challenge for the Jesuits. Since the murder of Isaac Jogues and his companions only twenty years before and a few miles away, Mohawk contempt for missionaries had cooled little. The priests were understandably wary. Plus, the Jesuits had to learn the Mohawk language from scratch.

To make matters worse, hostilities were far from over. In 1669, the Mohican advanced from the east and laid siege to Caughnawaga. Many were killed or wounded during the three-day battle. Young Tekakwitha joined Father Pierron and the other missionaries in tending to the wounded and dying. Reinforced from nearby villages, the Mohawk pushed back the Mohican, pursuing them into the woods where they slaughtered them in great number. Returning with a score of captives, they began a three-day victory celebration that included torture and execution of the prisoners. Pierron objected but was ignored. So the priests were left to instruct the Mohican captives as best they could in Christian doctrine and baptize them all before they died.

Baptism was the foundation of the Jesuit mission in New France—which is what the collection of settlements and missions from the St. Lawrence to the Great Lakes was called. The ultimate goal of the mission was to save souls. It was a good-hearted endeavor by missionaries fervently convinced that, once sufficiently catechized and baptized, the natives of this new land would be assured of heaven. Otherwise, left to their own ancestral traditions and culture, they were, in the understanding of these courageous priests, assuredly destined for hell.

St. Jean de Brébeuf, a North American Jesuit martyr and mentor to Isaac Jogues, writing in the 1635 issue of *The Jesuit Relations*, put it this way: "The joy that one feels when he has baptized an Indian who dies soon afterwards, and flies directly to Heaven to become an angel, certainly is a joy that surpasses anything that can be imagined."[2]

Young Tekakwitha was having a difficult time. She was attracted to these French priests who were so kind, so gentle, and so peaceful. In contrast, Mohawk men seemed hard, aggressive, and belligerent: traits essential to survival in a wild land. But Tekakwitha wanted what the Jesuits had, and the priests were more than happy to share their faith with this Mohawk-Algonquin girl. The trouble was, her uncle, the husband of the aunt with whom she lived, didn't approve. He despised the Jesuits and commanded Tekakwitha to stay away from them. Additionally, he felt it was time for Tekakwitha to start pulling her weight. That meant bringing home a husband.

The Mohawk were longhouse people: living in long, narrow structures of tied-together poles covered with tree bark, in appearance not unlike a modern Quonset hut. Each longhouse sheltered several families. The women ruled the roost, with each family presided over by a matriarch. When a woman came of age, she was expected to bring a husband to the longhouse to provide meat for the table and protection from enemies.

Tekakwitha's aunts pressured her to step up to her obligations. They even invited the son of a close family from a neighboring longhouse to visit. But when he did, Tekakwitha fled into the woods and refused to see him. She had heard from the Jesuits that some devout women of the Catholic faith would forswear marriage and devote themselves to the Christian God all their lives. She did not want a Mohawk man. She wanted to be like the Jesuits.

Around this time, in 1675, Jesuit Father Jacques de Lamberville showed up in Caughnawaga. After considerable begging, Tekakwitha got her uncle to allow her to go to Lamberville and to study catechism with him. In response to this, Tekakwitha's aunts harassed her with ridicule and threats of punishment. They made her do all the heavy lifting and the dirty work that nobody else wanted. They took away her rosary and would not admit her to the table when she refused to work on Sundays. She yielded to their ill treatment and submitted to their harsh demands, but steadfastly refused to take a husband.

On Easter Sunday the following year, at the age of twenty, Tekakwitha was baptized by Father Lamberville, taking the Christian name Catherine. The French pronunciation, mixed with the Mohawk accent, rendered the name "Kateri," by which she would be henceforth known.

Kateri remained in Caughnawaga another year, enduring mistreatment and humiliation at the hands of her disapproving family and neighbors. Nasty rumors about her spread. She was accused of sorcery and witchcraft, sexual promiscuity, and even cannibalism. Finally, at Lamberville's suggestion, Kateri fled to Kahnawake, on the south bank of the St. Lawrence River across from Montreal—a village where other native converts, mostly women, were gathered.

It was in Kahnawake that Kateri began to experience church: a community of like-minded believers who studied, prayed, and worshiped together. Church, the gathering of the baptized to practice faith in a unity of mind and heart, has been the fuel of the Spirit's fire since the start of Christianity. Kateri's faith soared. She developed a devotion to prayer, the Eucharist, and the cross.

Much of Catholicism and French culture, as presented by the Jesuits, was at odds with traditional Mohawk ways. However, the spirituality of the cross dovetailed neatly with Mohawk thought and practice. Facing continual hardships of cold, starvation, war, and the possibility of capture and torture, the Mohawk prepared for these eventualities with practices of deprivation, fasting, and subjecting their bodies to harsh treatment, hoping to harden themselves against the inevitable need to endure the worst. Both male and female Mohawk were known to lash themselves with switches or throw themselves naked into the snow. One practice that occasionally proved lethal was to cut two holes in the ice some distance apart and then attempt to swim under the ice from one hole to the other.

Graphic images of Christ's suffering were favorite teaching tools of the Jesuits, the crucifix being the foremost. The priests also maintained the practice, then common in Jesuit communities, of reading aloud from martyrologies—gruesome stories of the torture and death of martyred saints—during communal meals. Native converts listened in thrall. These images and stories spoke to their Mohawk experience.

Some women of Kahnawake had spent time with the Ursuline sisters in Quebec City and learned from the nuns how certain devout women in Italy and France practiced the severe self-mortification of the flagellants. These practices involved wearing painfully irritating clothes and bloodying themselves with whips.

Kateri and a few of the others decided to try out these penitential practices. They would meet in the woods to cut switches and flail themselves, sometimes leaving their bare shoulders bloody. One woman went so far as to throw herself into the icy St. Lawrence clutching her three-year-old child. The Jesuits were furious when they found out and strictly prohibited any further repetition of the activity. As was usual in the relationship between the natives and the priests, the priests were ignored and the practices continued.

None of this should have surprised the Jesuits, who themselves came to New France expressly because the missions of North America were the toughest assignments in the Society. Hardship, discomfort, and self-denial were the practices of holiness, a way to unite themselves with the suffering Jesus. The cross was the symbol of Jesuit spirituality. They were the men of the cross, missionary marines in the battlefield of faith.

Hardship, of course, is a relative term. What these erudite Europeans, many from aristocratic French families, endured as great hardship was just another day in the life of the rugged Mohawk. If the Mohawk were going to suffer for Christ, they would have to dig a lot deeper.

Kateri believed such suffering was barter for her own sins and the sins of her people. This was a real leap in understanding for her, as the Mohawk had neither concept of, nor language for, sin and penance. In Mohawk culture, it was customary to compensate the victim of wrongdoing, not punish the wrongdoer. Young Catholic Kateri had come a long way in embracing atonement and the need for personal penance to accomplish reconciliation and redemption.

Gifted with spiritual understanding, Kateri plunged into a life of doing good, dedicating herself to spiritual and corporal works of mercy taught to her by the priests. Kahnawake provided her with many opportunities. Conditioned by the loss of her parents and brother to smallpox, and her own bout with the disease, Kateri regularly tended to the sick and those afflicted with various ailments.

This was when her light really began to shine. Kateri had a healing touch. Her presence was sought by ailing members of the village. She exuded a warmth in which others found great comfort. The Jesuits were aware of her spiritual gifts and her virtue. People would come to the missionaries with their complaints; the priests would send them to Kateri.

Two of the priests, Claude Chauchetière and Pierre Cholonec, kept journals of their life in Kahnawake, including detailed accounts of Kateri's activities. These accounts were printed in *The Jesuit Relations*, a periodical published back home in France. *The Jesuit Relations* told heroic stories of New France and was used to drum up financial support for the missions. It was through this media that the legend of Kateri Tekakwitha grew. Romantic images of "the savage virgin" caught the European imagination, and the young Mohawk woman gained a following on the continent.

Tekakwitha's healing gift proved to be extraordinary, but the many hardships of her life, plus her rigorous self-deprivations, took a toll on her health, already seriously compromised by the early bout with smallpox. Two years after arriving at Kahnawake, she began to decline. She died on Wednesday of Holy Week, 1680.

Father Cholonec reported in his journal that, within minutes after her death, a strange transformation occurred. Tekakwitha's face, darkened and deeply scarred by the ravages of smallpox, became radiant and smooth. The malformations disappeared. She who had healed others was herself healed. Additionally, one can imagine that her eyesight was restored: "She who bumps into things" now clearly beheld the face of God.

The Mohawk believe that the spirit of a dead person remains in the community for some time, later departing along the star path of the Milky Way to the place where the spirits of the dead dwell. In keeping with this tradition, three members of the Kahnawake community reported encounters with Tekakwitha in the days following her death. Each time Kateri told her friends she was on her way to heaven.

It is also a Mohawk tradition that once a spirit departs, it is gone for good. There is no longer any connection between the living and the dead. But the Jesuits held the classic Christian belief in the dynamic communion between the living and the dead: that the prayers of the living assist the souls on their journey, and the souls of the faithful departed come to the aid of the living.

Armed with their faith, the Jesuits encouraged the converts of Kahnawake to seek intercession from Kateri. Stories of healings were reported to the priests. Father Remy, from the Lachine settlement across the St. Lawrence, gathered soil from Kateri's grave and mixed it with ashes from her burned clothing. With this he formed a salve to apply to the sick and even a kind of tea for them to drink. More healings were reported. One woman was even delivered from compulsive gambling. So effective were Father Remy's potions that the local bishop mandated that every rectory in the diocese keep a supply of the salve for healing purposes.

The cult of Tekakwitha spread to Europe, where her relics and intercession were used to effect healings. Although these miracles were anecdotal and undocumented, they persisted for generations. In 1884, the Third Plenary Council of Baltimore initiated her cause for sainthood. Pope Pius XII declared her venerable in 1943. In an act of generosity typical of his pontificate, Pope John Paul II decreed that all the storied healings effected by Kateri's relics and intercessions be counted as one bona fide miracle, leading to her beatification in 1980. One more miracle was needed for her to be canonized.

That miracle came in 2006. In the state of Washington, a five-year-old named Jake suffered from a severe bacterial infection that modern medicine had been powerless to stop. Doctors said there was no hope.

Jake's parents called for their priest to give him the last rites. Because Jake was part Lummi, they begged the intercession of Tekakwitha, engaging the community of Jake's friends and classmates to join their prayers. A religious sister, who had taken the name Kateri at her profession, visited Jake and pressed a bone relic of Tekakwitha against the boy's body while she prayed for the Mohawk's intercession. The next day doctors found the progress of the infection had stopped. Jake would live.

In 2011, Pope Benedict XVI accepted Jake's healing as the second miracle needed for canonization, and the following year the pope named her a saint, more than 332 years after her death.

Why did canonization take so long? Perhaps the idea of a saint outside the box of white European piety didn't catch on until fairly recently. Neither did it help that Kateri was a convert and a lay woman. These factors were subtracted from the equation of her sanctity in the minds of Church leaders needed to advance her cause. It wasn't until the cultural upheavals of the 1960s, followed by the pontificate of John Paul II, that the canonical net was cast beyond the saintly stereotype. By the turn of the millennium, Kateri's race and ethnicity had perhaps become a benefit rather than a detraction. The canonization of Mexican Indian Juan Diego Cuauhtlatoatzin in 2002, 454 years after his death, set the table for the elevation of Kateri to sainthood.

A fundamental doctrine of Catholicism is belief in the communion of saints, the spiritual community of believers alive in this world and the next. This "cloud of witnesses" is distinguished not by what makes them different, but what makes them the same. Christian faith transcends race, ethnicity, culture, gender, language—everything that divides and spurs conflict.

Saint Kateri Tekakwitha is a reminder that the mystical communion of divinity and humanity, realized in Jesus and manifested in the Church, is found in all people. This young Mohawk woman living in the forests of what would become upstate New York was as far removed from the Catholic mainstream of the seventeenth century as one can get and still be on the same planet, yet she believed and put her faith into practice.

Kateri became a saint for all people, but especially for those living beyond the boundaries of the familiar and acceptable. She is a saint for anyone willing to take the adventure of life all the way to the edge.

Today

The Mohawk People remain in southeast Canada and upstate New York. There is also a community of Mohawk ironworkers who live in New York City. Known for their fearlessness, they helped to build the Empire State Building and One World Trade Center. More than three hundred books have been published in twenty languages on the life of Kateri Tekakwitha. Her birthplace, Ossernenon, is on the grounds of the National Shrine of North American Martyrs in Auriesville, New York. Nearby, in the town of Fonda, is the National Shrine of Saint Kateri Tekakwitha. In Canada, a shrine to St. Kateri is located in the St. Francis Xavier Mission, in the Mohawk community of Kahnawake. Many churches, schools, and other institutions in the U.S. and Canada have been given her name.

Timeline

- 1646: Jesuit Martyrs Isaac Jogues and Jean de Lalande killed by the Mohawk at Ossernenon
- 1656: Tekakwitha born in Ossernenon to Algonquin mother and Mohawk father
- 1660: Smallpox epidemic kills Tekakwitha's family; Tekakwitha survives
- 1666: French destroy Ossernenon; community moves to Caughnawaga; Jesuits arrive
- 1676: Tekakwitha baptized; takes the name Catherine, rendered "Kateri" in Mohawk
- 1677: Tekakwitha moves to Catholic settlement at Kahnawake
- 1680: Tekakwitha dies at Kahnawake on April 17 at age twenty-four

3] Blessed Junípero (Miguel José) Serra
(1713–1784)
Father of the California Missions
Feast: July 1. Cause opened: 1949. Venerable: 1985. Beatified: 1988.

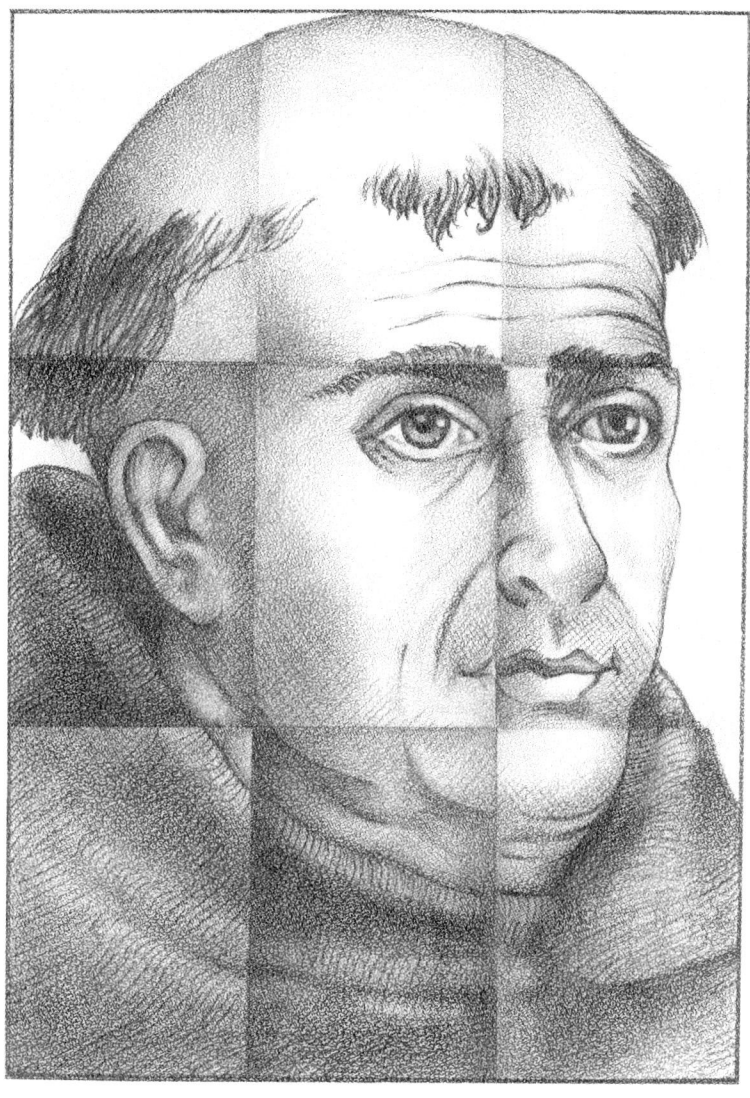

To die well…is our principal concern. For if we attain that, it matters little if we lose all the rest. And if we do not attain it, all the rest is of no value.[1]

The coastal cities of California have a Catholic sound to them. From San Diego to Santa Barbara, San Luis Obispo to San Francisco, the names of saints embroider the shoreline. They remind us that an aging and stubborn Franciscan priest brought the first sustained European presence to California. How he got there to "bequeath a necklace of missions"[2] to the territory is a long story, not without controversy. But Fray Junípero Serra was no stranger to conflict. You could say he was born to it.

To enter Serra's world is to take a giant step back into a moment of Church history that little resembles ours. Consider this: Francis of Assisi launched his mendicant ("begging") movement in the early thirteenth century. These mendicants owned nothing, liberating them to wander and preach, giving rise to a new era of vigorous apostolic activity. While the rest of Christendom frantically engaged in a Fifth Crusade against "the infidels," Francis was having respectful interfaith conversations with the Muslim Sultan of Egypt. Stories of Francis introduced a renewed passion for this sort of evangelical generosity: to bring the Gospel to "gentiles" who faced damnation, yet lived in perilous ignorance of the danger.

In Spain, the missionary movement found a particular fervor. It propelled secular men like Christopher Columbus to take two friars with him on his second voyage to the New World. Between 1493 and 1820, 8,500 Spanish Franciscans headed for the Americas. They entered Mexico with the explorers as early as 1505, planting missions in New Mexico, penetrating the interior as far north as Kansas, establishing a presence in Florida, and founding missions in Texas. None of these missions north of the present-day border were numerically successful, nor were they sustained very long due to native attacks that racked up martyrs for the Church most everywhere the friars went.

The dismal effort-to-achievement ratio didn't deter more volunteers from stepping forward. On the contrary: stories of martyrs in the mission fields engaged the religious imagination of fervent boys like Miguel José Serra on the Mediterranean island of Mallorca. Even as the Church rolled out newly minted saints and martyrs, the youth of Spain and its territories devoured the details of these holy lives, experiencing the personal electricity of a recruitment poster.

For Serra and his companions, life on an economically impoverished island like Mallorca offered no purposeful future. Bouts of famine and disease made family life an almost hopeless proposition. Escaping a claustrophobic island future to become heroes of the faith in the romantic haze of the mission lands must have seemed wonderful. A Franciscan training school for missionaries situated on Mallorca churned out candidates nonstop for New World ventures.

Serra entered the Franciscan order at age sixteen. His parents delivered him to the door of the school during a decade of famine, relieving themselves of another mouth to feed. Serra, for his part, was anxious to begin. He was saturated with the stories of heroes he felt compelled to imitate, like that of mystic Ramon Llull, a fifteenth-century Franciscan tertiary who believed the whole world could be converted to Christianity by reason alone. Llull had founded the school Serra was entering.

Then there was Fray Antonio Llinás, another Mallorcan who had been both missionary and founder of a missionary school in Mexico City, New Spain. Llinás in turn recruited Padre Antonio Margil de Jesús, who in Serra's lifetime preached throughout Central America, Louisiana, and into Texas; news of Margil's death reached Mallorca when Serra was thirteen.

Newly canonized Francis of Solano, the Apostle of Peru, dazzled Serra with the thousands he had baptized, the sick he had cured, and how he had even been known to predict the future. All of his life, St. Francis of Solano had maintained "a continuous martyrdom of penance, self-mortification, fasts, and afflictions against his body."[3] This brand of holy machismo became the blueprint for Serra as he grew to manhood.

Despite his parents' illiteracy, Serra could already read and write in two languages and had become a fine singer by the time he entered the order. He took the name Junípero to honor the companion of Francis of Assisi who was known for foolish behavior and simplistic wisdom. Like most else Serra would do, the name selection was motivated by deep humility. Serra was far from simpleminded. His professors were quickly impressed by his grasp of philosophy and theology. Within a decade Serra was back in the classroom, this time as a professor himself.

Serra taught his students that the intellectual life was necessarily grounded in the moral life. Only a moral person could become wise; learning was wasted on the ethically challenged. When his students graduated, Serra humbly submitted that he was no longer their teacher, but their servant. The class exploded in applause, and two of his students—Francisco Palou and Juan Crespí—would follow Serra the rest of their lives.

At age thirty-five, Serra was warmly regarded on Mallorca as a man of learning and a persuasive preacher of local missions. But in 1748 the yearning to follow his missionary heroes culminated in an interior call to go to New Spain. Serra tested it by praying that someone else in his community would experience the same call. Shortly afterward, Palou came to Serra with that idea in mind. By the new year, they, Crespí, and a band of other friars were off the island for the first time in their lives, bound for a world beyond their imaginings.

Anyone who has ventured outside of his or her cultural box might appreciate Serra's naiveté upon entering the wildly novel context of New Spain. On a stop in Puerto Rico, the boatload of budding missionaries got a chance to relay-preach a long mission. Serra, whose style was elegantly academic and well-reasoned, was stunned when the highly emotional, non-rational approach of another missionary had a far greater impact on their Puerto Rican audience.

Serra resolved to retool his method, and during his years in Mexico became famous as a popular, passionate evangelist. He beat his chest with a rock to open hearts to contrition, extinguished a candle against his skin to conjure up the pains of hell, and whipped his bared back with chains to do penance for the sins of mission attendees. His fellow Catholics in New Spain couldn't get enough of him.

Of course, Serra hadn't come halfway around the world to preach to Catholics. He had come to the New World to rescue heathen souls from certain perdition, a crystal-clear motive that drove most of his companions to dedicate their lives and surrender their deaths to the missions. What these altruists barely realized is that they were, at the same time, being used for other purposes: through the handy vehicle of the *patronato real*, the Spanish church had become more or less an empire-building tool of the Crown.

Spain needed missionaries to subdue and civilize the frontiers in advance of its settlements. The native peoples were to be transformed into Spanish-speaking, tax-contributing citizens of the Empire. Once that goal was accomplished, the government expected the friars to step aside. This precarious yoking of Church to state led to endless confrontations and crossed purposes.

Neither the civil authorities nor the missionaries considered the preferences of the native populations. Some of these heartily resisted the usurpation of their territories by conquistador and missionary alike. Others found profit in trade with the newcomers, sought similarities, and made accommodations. Some became convinced that the missionaries were their only allies against brutal conquering forces. And some would seek the consolation of the friars' new religion in a sea of changes which nothing in their native traditions had prepared them to navigate.

When Serra's party first arrived at Veracruz, Mexico, Serra elected to walk to the mission college in Mexico City rather than go on horseback like the rest. That two-hundred-fifty-mile journey instigated the infection in his leg that would plague him all his life, probably the result of mosquito or chigger bites on his sandaled feet. In future excursions the swelling and pain sometimes threatened the success of an expedition.

Serra always prayed his way beyond the malady or sought local healing interventions—once from a muleteer who knew how to treat lame animals. Serra's deep humility made it easy for him to seek help from any source. His zeal for saint lore also made it natural for him to embrace suffering as a channel of divine grace. Like St. Paul's "thorn in the flesh" that kept the apostle from pride, Serra's ulcerated leg became a peculiar mark of God's favor to him.

Serra's first mission among Native Americans was not to virgin territory, but to the Sierra Gorda region. Here he retraced the steps of friars who had already baptized local populations but failed to lure them to a converted way of life. Serra's task was to persuade the natives to stay in the settlements and to live "under the bell": governed by the summons of the mission bell to prayer, catechism, work, and meals.

The field guide of successful missions urged structured routines, agricultural labor, and discipline, augmented with corporal punishment to promote "devotion, decency, and good order" among native peoples.[4] In Spanish culture, loving fathers liberally applied the rod to their children; it didn't seem unreasonable to Spanish missionaries to treat the morally ignorant "gentiles" like children and to beat them.

Serra followed the book on missionary method. He doled out daily food rations along with blankets and clothing to entice the native peoples to the advantages of settlement life, and to discourage the roving rhythms of hunter-gatherers. Once inside the mission, they were catechized and introduced to European language and customs.

According to the numbers and buildings that measured missionary accomplishment, in eight years Serra was more successful in Sierra Gorda than previous friars had been. As a result, he was considered for a new assignment in Texas after a local rebellion destroyed a Franciscan mission there. But the appointment was repealed before Serra headed north: it was determined not advantageous to rebuild in Texas. Instead, Serra returned to the Franciscan college in Mexico City for another decade, teaching and offering local missions to Catholics as he'd done back in Mallorca. He might have remained just another Franciscan missionary in New Spain if not for the ill fortune of the Jesuits.

A tangle of events happened in a short timespan. New World realities were like that: regional setbacks set ripples in motion across vast territories. First, Spain lost Florida to the English. The Spanish government responded by strengthening its western holdings, and part of that reorganization involved expelling the Jesuits from New Spain. Portugal had gotten rid of its Jesuits in 1759; France had done the same in 1764. By 1767, Spain was ready to follow the trend. The Jesuits were singled out from other missionary groups because they were wealthier, more international, and more independent than other religious orders. That implied they were also harder to control.

When nearly three thousand Jesuits were suddenly eliminated from the mission territories, gaps opened everywhere for groups like the Franciscans to fill. Serra was assigned at once to take over the Baja (Lower) California missions that the Jesuits were forced to abandon. He and his missionary band had hardly arrived, however, when a Russian movement down the western coastline of North America alarmed Spanish authorities sufficiently to organize a completely new mission to Alta (Upper) California. This was precisely the "gentile" territory Serra had desired to serve all his life. At fifty-five, he was already old for a missionary, with at least two full careers behind him. Yet the mission he'd dreamed of had finally materialized, and he fervently seized it.

Spanish civil authorities ordered three missions to be founded in Alta California: at San Diego and Monterey, both known ports, and another in between, to be called San Buenaventura (near present-day Ventura). Serra's plan quickly surpassed that goal. He envisioned a complete staircase of missions, each three days apart, up and down the coast. Serra personally founded nine missions in the fifteen years he gave to the cause. Before the close of the California mission era, there would be twenty-one such sites in all.

If evangelization were a matter of numbers, Junípero Serra was easily the most successful missionary in the New World. His record number of mission sites, the thousands he baptized and confirmed, the spectacular success of his New World agricultural empire up and down the coast, and the enduring and beautiful structures he designed to the finest details and helped construct with his own hands are a testament to what is possible when an unquenchable optimist of clear convictions is given an open-ended commission.

In Serra's lifetime, Native Americans living at the settlements did enjoy a certain paternal protection from the less-altruistically motivated Spanish soldiers and settlers. Serra fought pitched battles with civil authorities to keep his baptized flock "under the bell"—and not under the more exploitative dominion of the conquistadors. But he couldn't keep the future from barreling in, with its dire consequences.

The missions reached a pinnacle of numerical and economic success under the friars after Serra's death in 1784. But these sites were soon subject to the secularization process that Spain dubbed the New Method, designed to sweep the Franciscans aside—as had been the plan all along. Natives at the settlements were released into the nominal care of parish priests brought in for the purpose. But most of the converts promptly abandoned parish life—with its thin material and social offerings compared with the full-service mission communities—for the old ways and customs.

Epidemic diseases were not unknown before the arrival of the Europeans, but many new ones were introduced. These were, unfortunately, more devastating than previous scourges for those who remained in the thickly centralized communities. Meanwhile, the addition of European livestock and their foraging habits wreaked havoc on local ecosystems, disrupting the gathering rhythms of native communities and driving them back into the settlements, increasing their vulnerability to sickness.

Over time, the settlements became the best of a series of worsening options for the native peoples. A smallpox epidemic in 1844 was followed by the brutality of wild-eyed gold-rush gamblers that same decade. Altogether, in under a century these factors reduced the 310,000 Native Americans of Serra's day to a population of 50,000. The dream of saving souls had unwittingly resulted in the decimation of entire cultures.

Serra died of heart failure, developed through a lifetime of wilderness deprivations, in present-day Carmel Valley at San Carlos Borromeo Mission. This was not how he had planned it; to be a martyr was the deepest desire of every missionary, not death in one's own bed due to the wear and tear of the years.

If Junípero Serra's life had ended violently at the hands of raucous solders or rebellious natives, rather than simply fraying from hard use at the age of seventy, he would most likely have been declared a saint shortly after his death. His remarkable courage, unflagging zeal, brilliant oratorical style, pioneering vision, and selfless sacrifices match the spirit of what was called holy in this period. Instead, Serra's cause had the misfortune to be delayed into an age that holds deep reservations about the mission programs of earlier centuries and even their fundamental objectives. In California, a place thinly inhabited by Native Americans today, a necklace of haunting and beautiful mission buildings still echo with questions in search of answers.

Today

Most of the twenty-one California missions still stand. Fifteen are within active parishes; one is a retreat center; two more have been named basilicas. Two are contained within state parks. Only one is in ruins. Serra's legacy is carried on through Serra International, which fosters and affirms vocations to priesthood and religious life in thirty-six countries. Serra was buried at the site of his home mission, San Carlos Borromeo, in Carmel.

Timeline

1565:	First Mass celebrated in the future U.S. at St. Augustine, Florida
1700s:	Florida missions destroyed by English takeover
1713:	Miguel José Serra born November 24 in Petra, Mallorca
1730:	Serra enters the Franciscans in Palma
1749:	Serra gives up professorship to join the missions in Mexico
1750–1758:	Serra takes over Sierra Gorda missions with Palou
1758:	Franciscan missions in Texas attacked
1758–1767:	Serra returns to College of San Fernando de Mexico and gives retreats

1767: Serra takes over Baja California missions after Jesuit expulsion
1769: Serra begins missions in Alta California
1776: Revolutionary War begins in the English colonies
1784: Serra dies on August 28 at Mission San Carlos Borromeo in Carmel at age seventy

4] Elizabeth Ann Bayley Seton
(1774–1821)

The Family Saint

Feast: January 4. Venerable: 1959. Beatified: 1963. Canonized: 1975.

The only word I have to say to every question is, *I am a Mother*. Whatever providence awaits me consistent with that plea I say Amen to it.[1]

Daughter. Wife. Mother. Convert. Teacher. Friend. Foundress. Saint. Whenever Elizabeth Seton was pressed to define herself in the rapidly shifting sands of her circumstances, the identity she claimed as her highest priority was Mother. She capitalized this word because to her it was an ultimate vocation, not to be dismissed or reduced. And Seton needed her fierce maternity amid entrenched Catholic structures that propelled her into a world normally circumscribed by vows and veils, celibacy and solitariness.

Make no mistake, Elizabeth Seton was a Mother: first, of the five children she bore with her husband, William; secondly, of the seven she inherited when her father-in-law died; thirdly, of the community she would lead as foundress of the Sisters of Charity of St. Joseph; also, to the children who populated her community's schools and orphanages and often resided with the sisters. Perhaps most of all, Mother Seton became the primary nurturer of countless seminarians and priests who became pastors of the newly established American church centered in Baltimore. If U.S. Catholicism has an Earth mother, it is Elizabeth Seton.

We don't have to look far into Seton's story to understand why motherhood was her signature vocation. Young Elizabeth Bayley lost her own mother at the age of three. She and two sisters, older Mary and baby Catherine, gained a stepmother the following year. But the second Mrs. Bayley would soon bear seven more children, and didn't warmly welcome the offspring of a previous marriage into her household. Baby Catherine died at age two; Mary and Elizabeth mostly lodged with an uncle outside of town.

Elizabeth's interior history was isolating, yet the exterior reality was not uncomfortable. The Bayleys inhabited the enchanted world of upper-class New York in the late eighteenth century, just before the Revolutionary War exacted its toll on the city. Members of the Church of England, educated and well connected, they hovered at the peak of the city's roster.

Elizabeth's mother had been the daughter of an Episcopal rector. Her father was a prominent doctor, public health advocate, and professor of medicine at King's College (later known as Columbia University). After his first wife's death, Dr. Bayley traveled a great deal presenting his research. He provided for his first family's education but spent little time with them. Adolescent Elizabeth wrote him longing letters expressing a desire to have her father closer.

Sensing a danger in his daughter's emotional dependency, Dr. Bayley advised her to become the mistress of her own person and to avoid "dysentery of the mind"—a phrase that came easily to a public health physician mired in cyclical epidemics. Elizabeth embraced his advice, developing a self-possession that would prove essential in the decades to come. If she had no personal champion, as every good parent is for a child, then she would become that champion for others. The motherless child would reinvent herself as über-mother for the world. Seton's lifetime genius for relationships was grounded in a need for belonging, rooted in her earliest years.

If "mother" was her primary vocation, courage in dealing with death was a close second. Love and grief are close companions. The decision to love implies a willingness to suffer for love's sake. The same intensity of devotion that Seton would invest in family, friends, mentors, novices, and students was also the source of her deepest anguish.

The eighteenth-century world, as her doctor-father could testify, was riddled with disease. Mysterious and poorly understood illnesses regularly swept through populated areas, carrying off young and old alike with a punctuating inescapability. In reading Seton's biographies, it's hard to shake the suspicion that death stalked Elizabeth with a particular vendetta. But it was nothing personal. Only a generation earlier, Emily Dickinson had described death's timeless pursuit in words that might have spoken directly to the mature Seton's heart:

Because I could not stop for Death—
He kindly stopped for me—
The Carriage held but just Ourselves—
And Immortality.[2]

Elizabeth Bayley rode along between Death and Immortality in her early losses of mother and sister. She endured death's sting again in her marriage to William Seton, who died of tuberculosis nine years later.

The match has been excellent by the standards of their fathers. Dr. Bayley and the elder Seton were both Crown loyalists even after the War led to the dramatic shift into nationhood in 1783. Anglicans, Presbyterians, Dutch Reformed, and Lutherans still kept tight control of the gates of respectability in New York, though the colony was now in the hands of an untested "United States of America." William's Tory father was so delighted by his new daughter-in-law that he named Elizabeth the guardian of his own children in the event of his death. Happily for her, the new Mrs. Seton adored her husband, with whom she bore her cherished brood: Anna Maria, William, Richard, Catherine Josephine, and Rebecca.

The founding of the new Republic planted the seed of a problem for the Setons. William's father held half-interest in a shipping firm with finances anchored in British trade. Four years into his son's marriage, the elder Seton died suddenly, leaving the company in the younger William's hands. Regrettably, William had far less business acumen than his father. In the same hour, Elizabeth inherited the care of her late father-in-law's seven dependent children. The young couple's household doubled overnight.

The eldest stepdaughter, Rebecca, at eighteen only a little younger than Elizabeth herself, became her sister-in-law's dearest and best ally. William didn't fare as well with his inheritance. Unable to gain control of the opaque dealings of the firm, William soon faced bankruptcy. Losing the business meant loss of home and status for the Setons: humiliatingly, even the furniture and children's clothes had to be listed with their creditors. Not long afterward, Dr. Bayley, Elizabeth's much-revered father, succumbed to yellow fever while treating victims of another outbreak. The loss of her father's steady counsel in this time of financial ruin was very keenly felt by Elizabeth.

The practice of self-possession was the one true legacy Elizabeth's father had left her, and it was invaluable. Her devotion to her family was unshakeable in their imminent social demotion. The spiritually unmoored William, however, could not bear the shame of failure. Haunted by specters of poverty and prison, his already precarious health entered a downward spiral.

In hopes that a warmer climate might restore William, the Setons decided to risk a voyage to Italy, seeking refuge with the Filicchis, longtime faithful business partners with the firm. They left the children under Rebecca's supervision, taking only Anna, their eldest, with them.

During the brutal weeks at sea, William clung to life. A final cruel obstacle awaited the Setons in Italy. Due to the yellow fever epidemic raging in New York, the Italian authorities were unwilling to permit the obviously ill William to enter their country. The family was quarantined in a damp and drafty offshore cell known as the Lazaretto—a confinement that hastened the end of William's life. Within this terrible imprisonment, husband and wife comforted each other by reading the Psalms and Isaiah, St. Paul and Revelation. William told Elizabeth repeatedly that, whether he lived or died, he would always consider this period of his life the most blessed, the only time he had not lost. Released a month later, the Setons were welcomed into the Filicchis' home at last, where William died.

Her young husband's death was traumatic. As a new widow, she was forced to bury her William in a foreign land, surrounded by strangers. Moreover, the religion of this place was the feared and deplored Catholicism that Elizabeth had been bred to mistrust. Despite the Filicchi family's sensitivity and graciousness, Elizabeth longed for her New York family and her familiar community. As the scheduled day of departure drew near, her daughter Anna developed scarlet fever. The same authorities that wouldn't permit William Seton to enter the country weeks earlier now refused to allow Anna to board the ship. Elizabeth was obliged to prolong their stay in Italy.

With many kindnesses, the Filicchis won Elizabeth's heart. She began to accompany them on small sightseeing trips around Italy, mostly involving shrines and churches. Despite herself, Elizabeth became fascinated with the frequent scenes of pilgrims on their knees before the Blessed Sacrament, enrapt with a certainty of the constant Presence of Christ in those holy places.

As a family of means, the Filicchis had a house chapel in which Mass was celebrated and the Real Presence was available for visitation at all hours. Elizabeth felt a growing hunger to experience such an intimate proximity to the Lord as these people professed to have. Just as the younger Elizabeth had once clung to human relationships as the survivor of a shipwreck grasps at anything that floats, the widow now found herself in a sea of bereavement reaching for a mystery in hopes of rescue.

In her classic biography of Elizabeth Seton, Annabelle Melville identifies the future saint as a woman of deep religious sensibilities who was also a woman of the Republic. This duality led to the period of searing confusion that accompanied Elizabeth back to the U.S. She was undeniably drawn to the strong, mystical expression of faith she'd witnessed during her sojourn among the Italians. All things being equal, she might have converted to Catholicism on the spot. But things were far from equal.

As a woman of the Republic in the early nineteenth century, flirting with Catholicism was social suicide. There was exactly one Catholic church in New York: seedy old St. Peter's on Barclay Street. It was "a horrid place of spits and pushing"[3]—a far cry from the magnificent Italian houses of worship that had so moved her. German, French, and Irish immigrants from around the city made their way to St. Peter's, "dirty, filthy, red-faced" folk who were "the off-scourings of the people,"[4] as Elizabeth confided frankly in her letters and journals. Mass at St. Peter's could even involve heckling by non-Catholics. The whole dreary experience presented to the doctor's daughter a clear picture that conversion also meant communion with a lower class of society.

Elizabeth's effusive writing habit provides us with front-row seats as she wrestles down the demons in her discernment. Her journal from Italy was kept for beloved Rebecca, the sister-in-law/step-daughter who held the family together in her absence. Sadly, Elizabeth and Anna had hardly returned from abroad when Rebecca died of tuberculosis. Her frail constitution had held on just long enough to say good-bye.

It was with Rebecca that Elizabeth had most wanted to share her revelatory experiences of Italy. How often had the two attended Episcopal services together, saying ruefully at the end: "No more until next Sunday." Rebecca alone might appreciate Elizabeth's discovery that the Catholics *always* had more with their daily Eucharist, this constant Real Presence, all the doctrines of the Blessed Sacrament that so astonished Elizabeth during her time among the Italians.

After losing Rebecca, her two younger sisters, Cecelia and Harriet, attached themselves to Elizabeth even more passionately. The widow had her own five little ones plus two inseparable stepdaughters requiring her constancy, yet she was obliged to live with a variety of relatives. It became essential for Elizabeth to procure an income. Her accomplishments and education suggested teaching, or perhaps a boarding school. She made several attempts in this direction, but each met the same challenge: Elizabeth's unseemly association with the Catholic Church was becoming a source of alarm for her relatives, her longstanding Episcopal mentor and pastor, and any who might entrust their children to Elizabeth's instruction.

Making a profession of faith was hardly a private matter in Seton's generation. The conversion of a woman of her social profile would be of great interest to the American Catholic Church as well. The well-connected Filicchis brought Elizabeth's struggle to the attention of John Cheverus, later a bishop of Boston, and John Carroll, already the first bishop of the new See of Baltimore. Both lent encouragement.

While gratified to have so many well-placed Catholic advocates, Elizabeth still faced crushing economic realities and bitter disapproval from those closest to her. One relative removed Cecelia and Harriet from her home, as both were showing an alarming interest in Elizabeth's Catholic sympathies. Elizabeth wavered in her resolve many times. In the end, however, she marched into St. Peter's Church and made her profession of faith, accepting the consequences. Bishop John Carroll himself came up to New York to confirm her.

It took another three years for Elizabeth to embrace the necessity of transplanting her family to Maryland. As Melville observes: "The convert is ultimately a citizen of a new state which precludes a return to his former soil."[5] In 1808, that "new state" was Baltimore: the third largest U.S. city and center of the American Catholic universe.

Baltimore had become the first U.S. diocese in 1789. In 1808, the American Church included four additional divisions called suffragan sees: Philadelphia, New York, Boston, and Bardstown, Kentucky. Baltimore contained twenty-five Catholic churches; the nation's first seminary, St. Mary's; and the new Georgetown College. Mount Saint Mary's College served as a minor seminary in nearby Emmitsburg. Most especially, John Carroll was in Baltimore, and he had plans for Mrs. Seton.

After procuring a promise that her sons would be educated at Mount Saint Mary's, and that her daughters would be included in any schemes for a Baltimore household, Elizabeth agreed to move. A house on Paca Street was located for her first Catholic school. Bishop Carroll received vows from Mother Seton as foundress of a new order, the Sisters of Charity of St. Joseph—but not a vow of poverty, which the mother of five dependents would not take. Bishop Carroll discouraged her future confessors from accepting any permanent vows from this woman whose primary allegiance would always be to her first family. Carroll freely admitted to others that he was collaborating with a saint, and seemed to appreciate the foolishness of tampering with sanctity.

Others shared the Bishop's exalted opinion. Bishop Cheverus of Boston marveled at Seton's personal holiness, later admitting he could not think of time spent with her "without a thrilling heart." Ambrose Maréchal, third Bishop of Baltimore after Carroll's death, described Seton's conversation as "bewitching." Her confessor and friend Simon

Bruté, later Bishop of Vincennes, Indiana, placed Seton on par with saints like Teresa and Frances de Chantal.

It wasn't just bishops who fell under the fascination of Elizabeth's dark-eyed gaze, startlingly direct speech, and witty intelligence. The Filicchi family never forgot her, keeping up a lifetime correspondence. Most of her New York family and friends eventually forgave the shock of her conversion, and a few even followed her into the Church.

Samuel Sutherland Cooper, a wealthy convert and seminarian, was sufficiently enthralled to purchase for Seton the Emmitsburg property, which became the permanent site of her community. After the move to Emmitsburg, the ministry of Seton's Sisters of Charity expanded to include a boarding school for paying students from all around the Eastern seaboard, and a free day school for local students of poorer families. Mother Seton conducted conferences and retreats for both students and sisters, translated spiritual works from French that were unavailable in English, and wrote her own treatises as well. Soon her sisters accepted invitations to run orphanages in Philadelphia and New York.

The territory of their influence grew to include the minor seminary at Mount Saint Mary's. The official assignment at the Mount was to care for linens, keep accounts, and attend to students in the infirmary; yet many future priests remembered the love and advice they received from Mother Seton. Her goal was to make them all better priests—even those already ordained. If she heard a priest give a half-hearted sermon, she confronted him afterwards. When a priest excused his delivery on the grounds that he hadn't spent much time preparing, Seton exclaimed: "O Sir, that awakens my anger! Do you remember that a priest holds the honor of God on his lips."[6]

Seton continued to ride in the solemn carriage between Death and Immortality throughout her dozen years in Maryland. Just before the move to Emmitsburg, her stepdaughters Harriet and Cecilia came from New York to live with her. Cecilia was already sick; both young women died within months of their arrival. Two years later, Seton's eldest daughter Anna also died after a deathbed profession into the community. Anna had been her constant companion in faith since the transforming period in Italy, and her death was almost more than her mother could bear. Even while Anna lay sick, Elizabeth's youngest, Rebecca, took a fall that led to four years of increasing disability until her death.

Mother Seton could view all the little graves of her children from her convent window. Sisters of her community were not spared in this brutal period; several surrendered to fevers, flus, and tuberculosis. Father Simon Bruté, officiating at these all-too-frequent funerals, encouraged his dear friend Elizabeth to look away from death and to reinvest in those who still needed their Mother. "Let us not refuse to live," he gently advised. "The most generous Saints desired to remain."[7]

In all stories of religious women obliged to answer to clerical superiors, some of the men are revealed as heroes and others as villains. Mother Seton had her share of both. Sulpician Fathers John Dubois, Louis William DuBourg, and Jean-Baptiste-Marie David—all early leaders at the Catholic college and seminary in Baltimore and Emmitsburg— served as spiritual advisers (and sometimes obstacles) of Seton and her sisters. The first two later became significant bishops in the lives of other American saints. One historian notes that, "for putting up with the harassment...of French male superiors [Seton] deserved canonization!"[8] Her group of American Sisters in Emmitsburg was never going to conform to the constraints of medieval European convent life as imported French clerics might prefer.

For perseverance despite scarcity, illness, and loss (and demanding Frenchmen), biographer Melville lauds the sisters' toughness: "Not every pioneer woman was the muscular, sun-bonneted Amazon that some latter-day artists like to recreate. There were these others, some in widow's caps, clasping a catechism instead of a rifle, giving soft instruction...[to girls] who would go out 'over our cities like a good leaven.'"[9] Like so many in her family and society, Mother Seton contracted tuberculosis in her final years. "I try to make my very breathing a thanksgiving," she wrote in a season when she could accomplish little more than breathe.[10] To those gathered around her deathbed she repeated:

"Be children of the church. Be children of the church."[11] Having climbed to the privilege of that communion, Elizabeth Seton couldn't bear for any of her children to be deprived of such a legacy.

Today

Mother Seton's Sisters of Charity were founded under the rule of St. Vincent de Paul's Daughters of Charity, started in 1633 to assist "the poorest of the poor." The American order united with the international community in 1850. Worldwide, 18,000 Daughters of Charity continue to work in the fields of education, health care, social, and pastoral services.

The National Shrine of St. Elizabeth Seton is at Emmitsburg, Maryland, where Seton lived and is buried. Mother Seton House on Paca Street in Baltimore offers tours of Seton artifacts. New York City also has a shrine to the saint at one of her original homes on State Street.

Timeline

1774: Elizabeth Ann Bayley born August 28 in New York City
1776: Revolutionary War begins
1777: Elizabeth's mother dies, leaving three daughters
1783: Last British troops leave New York City
1790: John Carroll of Baltimore consecrated first U.S. Bishop
1794: Elizabeth marries William Seton in the Episcopal Church
1800: William's company goes bankrupt
1803: Setons leave for Italy; William dies abroad at age thirty-seven
1804: Elizabeth Seton returns to New York; Aaron Burr shoots Alexander Hamilton
1805: Seton received into the Catholic Church
1808: Seton moves family to Baltimore and begins school
1809: Seton moves to Emmitsburg; begins Sisters of Charity
1812: Rule receives final approval; War of 1812 begins
1821: Seton dies January 4 of tuberculosis at age forty-six

5] Rose-Philippine Duchesne
(1769–1852)

The Woman Who Prays Always

Feast: November 18. Venerable: 1935. Beatified: 1940. Canonized: 1988.

Father Varin spoke to me again of *Holy Indifference and of the slowness* with which the works of God are accomplished. I think I answered him that, on the contrary, Holy Scripture represents God as *racing with giant strides*.... The Father laughed at my vehemence and agreed that I was right.[1]

The old woman, grey, toothless, and crippled by rheumatism, sat with her Sacred Heart sisters and prayed her rosary silently, tears splashing on the beads. After a lifetime of disappointments, she was facing one more. This was the bitterest: her long-held dream of being a missionary to the native peoples of America was passing her by. She was too old now, too sick, too useless for such a mission. What plagued the tough old nun most was this: she had become what she most feared—a person without purpose.

Meanwhile an animated young Jesuit shared plans for journeying to the Potawatomi settlement with the sisters chosen for the mission. He spoke of the four sisters who would accompany him, while the superior of the group softly used the number three. Finally, the priest understood the significance of elderly Mother Philippine's tears. He pointed to the old nun and protested: "But *she* must come, too. Even if she can use only one leg, she will come. Why, if we have to carry her all the way on our shoulders, she is coming with us. She may not be able to do much work, but she will assure success to the mission by praying for us. Her very presence will draw down all manner of heavenly favors on the work."[2]

The Jesuit stood his ground. Philippine would go to the Potawatomi, despite all objections. This triumph had been a long time coming, and was rare for a woman best viewed as the patron saint of failure.

Rose-Philippine Duchesne was born for success. As the eldest surviving daughter of a merchant family in Grenoble, France, she belonged to a class that had ridden the industrial age to great advantage. During the Enlightenment era (the century before the French Revolution of 1789), thinkers like Voltaire and Rousseau were on the rise and religious loyalties on the wane. In this age of reason, it seemed everything might be grasped with the proper education.

For bourgeoisie like the Duchesnes, life was sweet. Women of the age weren't expected to have opinions, nor to be intellectual partners to their husbands. They simply had to manage a household, raise children, and master parlor entertainments like music and drawing. Dutifully, Philippine donned full skirts and broad hats and went to soirees. Still, her younger sisters arranged marriages ahead of her. Philippine's appearance proved a difficulty: marred by childhood smallpox, she was no beauty. Tall, with a regal bearing and an attractive dowry, however, she wasn't unmarriageable. This wasn't Philippine's concern: her heart was set on the cloister.

Religious vocations were viral in her family. Two aunts, a sister, and a half-dozen cousins and nieces went to the convent. Philippine had longed to join the Visitation nuns at Sainte Marie, overlooking Grenoble, since she'd prepared for First Communion there. When her father learned of this, he withdrew her from the influence of the sisters. However, Duchesne's most willful daughter didn't surrender so easily. One day Philippine convinced a sympathetic aunt to chaperone her to Sainte Marie just to speak to the nuns. Once there, the girl refused to leave. Her unhappy aunt was obliged to make an explanation to her parents.

Philippine made her escape from the secular world at age nineteen. It was 1888, a year before severe weather, unemployment, and starvation would catapult the French peasants to revolt. Soon the Bastille was stormed, and bourgeoisie like the Duchesnes supported a new social order—at least initially. They didn't want the same justice the peasants did, of course. Inevitably the privileged class appreciated that the revolution was coming for them, too, and most switched sides.

Philippine wasn't ignorant of the divide between rich and poor in her city. Ladies were expected to dabble in charities that kept the poor in their place. They weren't trained to take a more active role in social issues, however. So Philippine focused on the moral practice proper to women of her century: the perfection of the interior self. Destined for nurturing roles, pious women were devoted to adoration of the Eucharist—the ultimate source of nurture, as historian Catherine Mooney notes. Night adoration was popular among devout sisters, and Philippine was a champion of such vigils. A student of hers scattered bits of paper into the folds of Philippine's habit as she knelt rapt in prayer through the night, to betray any movement. The papers were undisturbed the next morning.

The Church cultivated distinct spiritual avenues of piety. Men were summoned to active exterior responsibilities. For clergy, that meant leadership, preaching, mission, even martyrdom. Men in religion called society to account for its failings and facilitated its repentance. Church women were to identify those failures in themselves and root them out. They accomplished this through customary practices: self-denial, seclusion, fortitude in sickness, and marathon bouts of prayer. Along the route of perfection, it was all the better if they supported the clergy, instructed children, and nursed the sick.

The cloister rule was meant to assist women in their desire to become beautiful souls for God, and Philippine ran shining rings around her companions in conforming to the rule. Ironically—perhaps suspiciously—she was the queen of humility. This was Philippine's biggest problem: immoderation in all things. Her steely will easily inclined toward a magnificent lowliness. Her vigorous self-abnegation demonstrated what Sacred Heart biographer Louise Callan termed a "high disdain for obstacles."[3] This made Philippine impatient with those who enjoyed a greater tolerance of their own imperfections.

Philippine's overwhelming righteousness made for trouble in communal life. She was a racehorse distressingly yoked to pack mules.

The French Revolution brought interior self-absorption to a shattering halt. Monasteries and convents were shuttered, Church land confiscated. Even cloisters like Philippine's, that offered practical services like teaching and nursing, were disbanded for the crime of assisting "refractory priests"—clergy who withheld allegiance to the new state. Philippine had longed to abandon the world. Yet four years after she entered Sainte Marie, the world had come looking for her.

When her cloister was closed, Philippine reentered society, but from a new angle. For the next twelve years, she experimented with reinvention. She and a cousin, likewise forced from a cloister, tried to live their old rule together in the family home. Their inconvenienced clan didn't approve. Meanwhile, reports from Grenoble made Philippine uneasy. Her old cloister was now a prison, filled with refractory priests. Children formerly in schools and orphanages ran ungoverned in the streets. Priests who hadn't fled or been jailed were in hiding, while people died without benefit of the sacraments.

Philippine returned to Grenoble for the priests. She tended them in prison and nursed them through typhoid fever. She also aided hidden priests and connected them clandestinely to the dying. Soon she had entered enough neighborhoods to have an intimate view of how the poor actually lived. She organized Ladies of Mercy to instruct poor children and tend to the sick. Her entrance into the reality of poverty remained with Philippine later in Midwest America, as she served among Creoles, Native Americans, African slaves, orphans, and the never-ending sick. In revolutionary France, she became a bridge between bourgeois wealth and the world's need.

Philippine inhabited a multitude of paradoxes. The same woman driven to contemplative life was governed by a vigorous nature that kept her hands active and dirty. Too independent to be a follower, she shuddered at assuming leadership roles. She loved the outdoors but hungered for a tiny world tucked behind a cloister grille. Unyieldingly willful, she preferred the structured world of the convent. Deep affections bound her to people and places, while her desire for mission lands tore her away from all she held dear. Most of all, this hard-headed woman, loath to spend a dime on practical things, would regularly throw barrels of money at unlikely programs for the poor and aid to tattered missionaries.

The missionary angle was especially complicated. By definition, those who choose cloistered seclusion do not go on foreign missions. For Philippine, who had heard stories of missionary Jesuits since childhood, the hope of joining them outweighed the absurdity of the idea. Also, females were not intended to be missionaries. A century later, people would still dismiss Frances Cabrini for expressing the same desire. Philippine actually didn't anticipate being an evangelist. It would have been her joy just to do Jesuit laundry and make altar linens to support their work among *les sauvages*, the primitive peoples of America.

Eventually, her secular Ladies of Mercy caught the attention of revolutionaries and were disbanded. Philippine briefly joined some ex-nuns who secretly practiced a weak version of their old rule, but half-measures disgusted her. She returned to Grenoble, determining that charity could not be ornamental in her life; it had to be the centerpiece. She resolved to move in two directions: to Mass when she could find it, and to the bedsides of the sick. Christ was visible to her in both places.

When revolutionary fervor cooled in France, Philippine determined to reopen the cloister at Sainte Marie. She managed to do it by 1801, bending her secular-minded father, several priests, and civil dignitaries to her goal. Philippine fully expected her former sisters to flock back when she swung open the gate, but they did not. A few did return, but no one stayed long. Ten years as a prison had taken its toll on Sainte Marie. Also, a dozen years back in bourgeois comforts made these former nuns accustomed to ease. They didn't want to give up their possessions, resume the burdensome rule, or accept the confines of the grille. Philippine, naturally, could abide no milder standard.

Then a priest ally recommended a new group to Philippine: the Ladies of the Faith, organized by the Fathers of the Faith—covert ex-Jesuits led by Joseph Varin. Anything Jesuit-sponsored was a magnet for Philippine, who agreed immediately to meet with the superior of these Ladies, Madeleine Sophie Barat. Father Varin lured Barat to the meeting with Philippine at Sainte Marie using these words: "You will find some companions there—especially one. Were she alone and at the remotest corner of the world, you should go after her."[4]

Sophie Barat's brother Louis had been a Jesuit before the Society's suppression in 1764. During the Revolution, Louis pushed Sophie through a priestly formation in theology and Scripture, preparing her for a special calling. Fathers Barat and Varin believed post-Revolutionary France would be redeemed by educating girls, the mothers of the future. Small and shy at twenty-five, Sophie became the superior of what was later known as the Society of the Sacred Heart of Jesus. She'd never seen a cloister before she went to meet Philippine at Sainte Marie in 1804.

Philippine was tasked in this encounter to start from scratch at age thirty-five. She prostrated herself at Sophie's feet and kissed them, quoting Isaiah: "How beautiful on the mountain are the feet of those who bring good news!" These women took the measure of each other's dedication and shared an instant recognition. The elder cheerfully submitted to the younger.

Talented and charismatic Mother Barat saw that changes were inevitable at Sainte Marie. The grille had to go; Sophie felt certain austerities made a religious worse, not better. She accepted no disciplines that didn't show spiritual fruits in the practitioner. If Philippine hadn't given Sophie Barat her absolute confidence, the changes would have been intolerable. Philippine's devotion was so complete that she could take to heart this advice from her new Mother: "Do not get downhearted about your faults, even if you commit a hundred a day. Draw from them, instead, an increase of humility and confidence."[5]

Within a year Mother Barat left Saint Marie to organize other houses. Philippine was burdened with unwelcome administrative duties for the next decade. In 1814, Napoleon was defeated, imprisoned Pope Pius VII was liberated, and the Jesuit order was restored. Philippine soaked up reports of new Jesuit missions, her fire to join them rekindled. She confided her missionary dream to Mother Barat and received a surprising admission: Sophie too longed for a missionary life, but had accepted that her life's work was in France. Before she died, Mother Barat would be the superior of three thousand women dispersed across four continents. Her only adventures would be lived through them.

In 1815, Mother Barat called delegates from all Sacred Heart households to meet in Paris. Philippine represented Sainte Marie at this council, not suspecting when she left Grenoble that she would never see her cloister again. The council decided to open a house in Paris; Philippine was commissioned to oversee the preparations. The move to Paris put Philippine in close range of Louis Barat, who fanned her missionary zeal. Without consulting his sister, Barat made arrangements with Bishop Louis William DuBourg of Louisiana for Philippine to open a Sacred Heart house in his diocese.

Bishop DuBourg pleaded his cause before Mother Barat personally. He knew Philippine longed to work with *les sauvages* in America. His diocese extended from Mississippi to the Rocky Mountains and he assured Sophie that Indians roamed across it. The bishop promised generous funding for a mission. He had a house in St. Louis waiting for her sisters.

DuBourg was a great solicitor of religious communities for his incomprehensible territory, but he rarely had the means to deliver on his promises. This Bishop DuBourg was late of Baltimore and an associate of Mother Elizabeth Seton. His unpredictability in that relationship might have factored into Mother Barat's discernment had she been aware of it. Philippine's relatives, in fact, would finance much of the Sacred Heart mission to America in the years ahead.

In 1818, at the age of forty-eight, Mother Philippine left Paris, bound for America, with four sisters: Octavie Berthold, Eugénie Audé, Catherine Lamarre, and Marguerite Manteau. The latter two had teaching experience; the rest would serve in administrative roles. None spoke English. Mother Barat didn't tell Philippine she was to lead the mission until the last moment. The thought made Philippine heartsick all the way to the New World, and was worse for her than the contaminated water, rotting food, ship-deck fire, and bout with pirates they had to contend with during the voyage.

In the bayous of Mississippi, the sisters saw Native Americans for the first time. They were not the noble savages Philippine was expecting. By the early nineteenth century, demoralized by loss of land and culture and decimated by disease, many Indians were also crippled by exposure to alcohol. This first glimpse of *les sauvages* was of sad, defeated men, who nonetheless bore a dignity that compelled respect.

Disembarking in New Orleans, there was no sign of Bishop DuBourg. Ursuline Sisters extended a warm welcome, and in the weeks ahead, these good sisters did everything possible to persuade the French sisters to stay in New Orleans, where language, culture, and climate would not be as daunting as conditions in the north. Philippine had contracted scurvy on the voyage, and was forced to go to bed and practice patience. Her fever, the stinging insects, and the suffocating heat did not sell New Orleans to her. Someone convinced her St. Louis was mosquito-free.

After more than a month without word from her bishop, Mother Philippine resolved to take her sisters north. The Ursulines insisted on paying for their travel. It took forty days on a steamboat up the Mississippi, plagued by mechanical failures, sandbars, and flood debris, to arrive in St. Louis. They found a town of 4,500 settlers, French in character, with agriculture and trade comprising its economy. What Philippine didn't find in St. Louis was more to the point: no convent awaited them. *Les sauvages* were also conspicuously absent.

Bishop DuBourg met with Philippine and dismissed her concerns: "But you did not expect to live in St. Louis, did you?" That had been the agreement in France; it was precisely what Philippine expected. The bishop insisted the sisters would be better off in St. Charles on the far side of the river, a place rich with potential for a school. He told her that one day St. Charles would be a major trade route between the East Coast and China!

Philippine's sense of geography was no better than her bishop's. She reluctantly accepted the new plan. It was bitter to be among settlers and Creoles rather than the Indians she'd longed to serve. Philippine wrote to Mother Barat that St. Charles might be the tomb in which the mission would be buried. An exchange of letters took up to a year to pass between the Midwest and France. This made every decision a lonely one for Philippine. By the time she received her superior's advice, it was well beyond too late.

The sisters rented a house in St. Charles. In one weekend, it was transformed into a convent, school, and chapel for their new enterprise.

They followed the French model of opening two schools at once: a boarding school with tuition, and a free day school for the poor. Philippine ran the free school, which drew twenty students the first month. The ignorance of frontier children astounded her. They knew nothing of God, Jesus, or hell. They didn't know the alphabet or when to say Amen! Poor students and paying ones were equally uninformed. Philippine's letters to Mother Barat were filled with indignant passages about drunk fathers and clotheshorse mothers who didn't know or care that their children were illiterate. The parents knew so little themselves.

Yet the children wound themselves around Philippine's heart. There were always more of them than money to run the programs. The river between St. Charles and St. Louis was a great obstacle: storms, floods, and ice often made the school inaccessible. The well went dry the first winter. They had apples but no bread—not even the American kind made of corn meal. Laundered linens set before the fire hung there frozen. Meanwhile the bishop still had the seven thousand francs they had brought from France and entrusted to him for their use.

There was so much to learn in America, English foremost on the list. Philippine, already fifty, learned how to read and understand it but was never confident enough to speak it. This increased her loneliness. The French sisters that had journeyed with her eventually became superiors of their own houses. Philippine could teach the Creole children who spoke French, but no others. She was alienated from English-speaking postulants who joined the order. She poured out her soul to her friend Sophie Barat in letters that preserve a priceless record of frontier life.

Missouri was still a territory when the sisters arrived. It became a state of the Union in 1820, one that allowed slavery. This led to some soul-searching for Philippine, who had left a country burdened by class to embrace a land bedeviled by race. The bishop instructed her not to mix the races, neither among her students nor her sisters, at the risk of destroying her schools. This was America's paradox: a land that denounced the injustice of European class society but accepted racism comfortably.

Philippine had to learn that Creoles and "half-breeds" were acceptable students—but not blacks and Indians. Philippine would have been glad to provide separate schools for each group, and to accept them as postulants too, if only in especially established third orders. Most of her plans were not approved in her lifetime. Even Mother Barat in France feared the loss of the entire enterprise if her sisters broke the social code.

Philippine became furious when encountering racism in an American-born postulant: "I answered her that they have the same soul as she; that they have been redeemed by the same blood and received into the same Church."[6] Still, when her sisters opened foundations in Louisiana, they were given slaves along with the households. In 1830, even Philippine in Missouri accepted a slave in lieu of tuition.

Slaves in Sacred Heart households were treated much like servants in France. They were permitted to take vows with the sisters each year, appeared in community photographs, and at death got the same circular notices to all the households as when a sister died. Philippine personally instructed the children of household slaves and nursed them and their parents when ill. With abolition, as with the French Revolution, however, she abstained from direct political engagement.

The St. Charles venture failed within a year. Bishop DuBourg then recommended a more accessible location: his own property in Florissant, closer to St. Louis on the right side of the river. Philippine had dismissed Florissant earlier and Mother Barat opposed it. But to Florissant they went, finding the bishop's house inhabited by a priest, Father De La Croix. To his credit, La Croix moved into the corncrib and gave the house to the sisters.

The bishop started construction on new buildings, promising "the greater part of the money" for the project. But being overextended with a new cathedral and seminary, he couldn't oblige. While still holding the sisters' francs, DuBourg forced Philippine to sign for a loan from a sharkish lender. At ten percent interest, Philippine was soon in over her head. The more practical Mother Barat eventually paid off the loan for her.

The Florissant house became as precious to Philippine as Sainte Marie had been. As a school, Florissant had strong moments, but was never out of the red. There were always more poor students than paying ones. The location was still off the beaten track, and the failing economy wasn't suitable for investing in children. While Octavie Berthold and Eugénie Audé both learned English well enough to teach, the other sisters muddled along. Philippine couldn't conduct business in English or make contacts to support her establishments. It mortified her that "God has not bestowed on us the gift of tongues."[7]

Philippine revered Bishop DuBourg and tried to rationalize his inconstancy. DuBourg became increasingly unpopular with Catholics in St. Louis, including the Jesuits who also received a bait-and-switch invitation to his diocese. In 1821, DuBourg decided to move back to New Orleans, where earlier adversaries had had time to mellow. Focused now on the southern portion of his diocese, the bishop lobbied for Sacred Heart sisters to occupy a house in Opelousas, Louisiana, also known as Grand Coteau.

The proposal sounded wonderful: a wealthy woman was offering her house, land, furniture, and travel expenses for the sisters to use as convent and school. What wasn't said was more important: Grand Coteau was isolated, under-populated, and had nearly non-existent transportation. The sisters would have limited access to a priest. Also, the woman offering the house expected to continue to live there and do her entertaining. Still in the dark, Philippine sent Eugénie Audé to open the mission there. More sisters were expected from France "soon." It took another eight months for them to arrive.

Despite all the obstacles in Grand Coteau, Eugénie triumphed as an administrator. The new school was debt-free in a year. Unhappily, Eugénie lost confidence in Mother Philippine's leadership and wrote to Mother Barat, asking for permission to be answerable only to France. The American mission developed a significant fracture that eventually broke it into splinters.

It is uncontestable that Philippine wasn't a practical administrator. She loved the poor too dearly to make any decision that did not put them ahead of every other consideration. She clung to the idea of keeping sisters in St. Charles to run a free school without a paying academy to cover its expenses and, in fact, did reopen St. Charles later on. She held onto Florissant long after it was clearly a financial sinkhole.

In 1827 her new bishop, Joseph Rosati, and Mother Barat both persuaded her to open an institution in St. Louis, intended to support the other two Missouri locations she stubbornly maintained. The timing was bitterly wrong. There were too few paying students, Catholics were indifferent, Protestants were hostile, debts grew, and banks folded in a national banking crisis. None of this had anything to do with Philippine. She did, however, trust clergy too much and herself too little. During thirty years on the frontier, her letters bemoaned how badly placed she was as a superior and how much she wanted just to pray.

Sophie Barat would have none of it. In France, she was disenchanted with the spiritual bankruptcy of the postulants coming to her. Philippine was a saint with a heart plumb-lined to the poor Christ. Barat feared another superior might content herself to be the administrator of successful schools. The Society of the Sacred Heart existed to bring the passionate divine love to the world: it wasn't about opening academies. Philippine's students wrote about the radiance that shone from Philippine's face when she came from chapel, "softer than sunshine." That meant more to Barat than the financial bottom line.

Philippine remained a hopeless administrator. She persistently ran schools that were top-heavy with non-paying students. She ran an unofficial flophouse for missionaries passing through the territory, feeding and keeping them and sewing full Jesuit habits for them out of material she scrounged from other projects. She wandered through the house at night, mending the clothes and shoes of students and sisters. She herself cleaned the outhouse, sat up with the sick, and kept night-long prayer vigils.

Yet priests who served as confessors for her sisters sowed dissent against Philippine privately. Spiritual directors denied her communion or absolution to force her obedience when nothing else could derail her stubborn purpose. To the priest who threatened to take back his altar from the chapel if she did not bend to his decision, she threatened to remove the tabernacle, which she had paid for. Both Bishops DuBourg and Rosati undercut her authority at various times by making deals with her subordinates.

If Philippine had remained in a French-speaking country, or behind a grille, or had the unqualified support of superiors and clergy, she might have made a different sort of leader. Even her closest friend Sophie Barat quietly sided with the bishop or other sisters over Philippine in certain matters, hobbling her authority at a fundamental level.

The trail of her failures lengthened. As the missions in Louisiana grew to three, Philippine lost control over them. The Southern communities themselves began to clash, threatening the success of all of them. Eventually, administrative genius Eugénie Audé went back to France in 1833, suffering an apparent loss of nerve. Octavie Berthold, Philippine's closest companion from the original mission, developed mouth ulcers which turned cancerous; she died in 1833. Bishop DuBourg had already returned to France in defeat in 1826. Disparaged and financially limping, Philippine persevered in Missouri.

An Indian school the Jesuits co-founded with Philippine at Florissant failed to thrive and was short-lived. As the government bought up Indian land, tribes were being pushed westward, and they took their children from the school as they left. The only way to minister to *les sauvages* was to go west with them. Philippine was anxious to do just that, but permission from France was not forthcoming.

At age sixty-five, Philippine was relieved as superior of the St. Louis house, and she retired to Florissant gratefully. Her missionary flophouse was bringing her wonderful guests: Stephen Badin, the first priest ordained in the New World; Bishop Flaget of Bardstown, Kentucky; and Bishop Bruté of Vincennes, Indiana. They dubbed Philippine the Francis of Assisi of the Sacred Hearts, another Teresa, and compared her with Francis Xavier.

While her hospitality was great, Philippine herself appeared in patched habit and veil. Though she never had money for anything else, she always managed a donation to these missionaries before they left her. As finances worsened, Mother Barat advocated closing the Florissant house. Philippine pleaded that the sisters there were useless anywhere else. She slept in the cubbyhole under the stairs to make space for sisters needing to convalesce. Other houses sent her their tubercular, mentally ill, or exhausted sisters. Others came just to be around Philippine's sanctity, apparent to those who had been her students or novices.

As early as 1835, Bishop Rosati began to advocate with Mother Barat for the long-awaited Indian mission. Five years later, Rosati moved to Rome before the mission advanced. The Potawatomi tribe in Sugar Creek, Kansas, had invited Jesuits in the territory to send Black Robes to them. The Potawatomi had previously been evangelized and many were already Catholic. This brought young Jesuit Peter Verhaegen to the parlor of the Sacred Hearts, to escort the chosen sisters to Sugar Creek. It was the hour Philippine had awaited all of her life, and thanks to a hundred small acts of charity toward missionaries, she was included.

Her triumph didn't last. The patron saint of failure was very sick at the mission's launch, and she lasted just a year at Sugar Creek. Most of the time, Philippine was too ill to do more than pray and, occasionally, to visit the bedsides of the dying. "She is just here to suffer," her fellow sisters noted.[8] Yet the Potawatomi revered the elderly, and took this old woman to their hearts. They called her *Quah-kah-ka-num-ad,* Woman Who Prays Always.

Philippine was valued by those who didn't idolize productivity of the ordinary kind. They knew this old one was good: she loved, and her presence had healing authority. To the Potawatomi, such presence was better than deeds. They drew near Philippine as she prayed, and touched her clothes to "take grace."

At the end of the year, Father Verhaegen was summoned to escort his elderly friend back to Missouri, which he did reluctantly. Philippine embraced her diminishment. She returned to St. Charles and spent another decade fading away. Her voice weakened, as did her eyesight.

She could no longer sew. She took the sacristy for her bedroom, moving only from bed to sanctuary. Her faults remained, obvious as ever. She was stubborn. She spoke too impulsively. Her rough ways often damaged the thing she was trying to fix. *"Je ne suis rien, je ne puis rien, je ne sais rien,"* she wrote in her prayer book: "I am nothing, I can do nothing, I know nothing."⁹ Verhaegen arrived in time to give her the last sacraments, and to offer her funeral Mass. Like all of Philippine's admirers, he saw something in that "nothing" that the world could use.

Today

Twenty-five hundred sisters of the Society of the Sacred Heart serve in forty-one countries, offering the heart of an educator as teachers, social workers, counselors, and medical personnel in settings as diverse as schools, parishes, hospitals, shelters, and prisons. First opened in 1818, the Sacred Heart Academy in St. Charles still emphasizes the community's five core goals: faith, intellectual values, social action, community, and personal growth. The Shrine of St. Philippine Duchesne is on the grounds of the Academy and includes a small chapel where Mother Philippine's body rests.

Timeline

- 1769: Rose-Philippine Duchesne born in Grenoble, France on August 29; Daniel Boone begins westward adventures
- 1788: Duchesne enters cloister at Saint Marie
- 1792: Cloister closed by French Revolution
- 1804: Duchesne received into new order of Ladies of the Sacred Heart
- 1818: Duchesne chosen for Missouri mission
- 1820: Missouri admitted into the Union
- 1821: Lower Louisiana foundation opens in Opelousas
- 1827: City House opens in St. Louis
- 1840: Duchesne removed as superior
- 1841: Sugar Creek mission among the Potawatomi begins
- 1842: Duchesne returns to St. Charles
- 1852: Duchesne dies in St. Charles on November 18 at age eighty-three

6] **Theodore (Anne-Thérèse) Guérin**
(1798–1856)
Pioneer Educator and Peacemaker
Feast: October 3. Venerable: 1992. Beatified: 1996. Canonized: 2006.

Pray for me occasionally that I may not lose courage; nay, more, that I may be brave enough to hold up others who falter sometimes.[1]

"What can a woman do to help?" A suitor challenged young Anne-Thérèse Guérin with this question, hoping to discourage her from entering the convent. Anne-Thérèse had wanted God to make use of her since she had made her First Communion. But perhaps a poor woman living in the countryside of Brittany, France, was of no use to anyone. Anne-Thérèse mentally reviewed the unique contributions of Mary of Nazareth; biblical heroines Judith and Esther; powerhouse saints Catherine of Siena, Clare, and Teresa. It seemed the young man with romance on his mind was mistaken. A woman could do a great deal to help!

Willing service was sorely needed in her generation. By 1799, the French Revolution had ended. Napoleon returned to France. Catholic clergy that hadn't fled or been killed during the years of suppression were coming up from the cellars. Yet times were still uneasy for the Church.

Guérin's parents had been united in love, but divided by their nation's bitter conflict. Laurent Guérin was an officer in Napoleon's navy; Isabelle's family was royalists. Their two sons died early. Isabelle had raised the girls, Anne-Thérèse and Marie, while Laurent was off waging war. Coming home on leave with considerable wealth on his person, Laurent was robbed and murdered near Avignon. At fifteen, Anne-Thérèse found herself the sole support of a widowed, broken mother and nine-year-old sister. Her dream of joining the Carmelites derailed, and she became a seamstress.

Five years later, when the need at home was not so urgent, Anne-Thérèse dared to speak of her vocation. Isabelle responded by encouraging young men to call. Isabelle wasn't going to lose her most useful daughter to a cloister. Ever obedient, Anne-Thérèse waited another five years, then begged for permission again. This time her mother relented. Times were changing. By 1823, the Church of France was rising from the ashes. Twenty-eight new religious orders were restoring the faith by taking up the instruction of the next generation.

During the Revolution, education had been scarce. Anti-elitist mobs had demolished many schools. Isabelle Guérin had taught her daughters at home. Later a cousin who was a theology student boarded with the family. He took on the intellectual preparation of Anne-Thérèse. This education proved invaluable when Anne-Thérèse encountered the Sisters of Providence of Ruillé. Their order was founded by a priest ordained secretly during the Revolution.

Once he could work openly in 1801, this Abbé had gathered stones with local children to build a school. He also collected young teachers who took the usual vows—poverty, chastity, obedience—and two more: to educate poor girls and care for the sick. The plan was simple: the sisters would open tuition schools for those who could afford it. These would, in turn, finance free schools for the poor. The Sisters would operate pharmacies that, by the same method, would dispense medicines to the poor at no charge. The local Bishop of Le Mans championed the Providence community as it gradually restored hope to his degraded diocese.

When Anne-Thérèse joined the sisters at Ruillé, she received the name Theodore. After a short novitiate, she became the superior of a household at Rennes. The town had a reputation for lawlessness; the girls placed in Theodore's care were deemed incorrigible. The sisters at Rennes offered a basic education, some life skills, and religious instruction to their charges, but they had been unable to reach these wayward girls, who were hostile to authority of any kind.

Sister Theodore began by breaking the classroom switch to bits, laying out the pieces in front of the students. She understood these girls had little experience of justice and less of genuine love. Attempts to break their spirits with punishments wouldn't help. She resolved to love them into obedience. Then she could lead them to learning, and finally to faith. In just a few sessions, the girls placed themselves in Theodore's hands, and before long she had their parents, too. For eight years, Theodore was a greatly beloved figure in Rennes.

Sister Theodore was affectionately close to her superior in Ruillé, Mother Mary. But rumors of insubordination implicating Theodore reached Mother Mary, who abruptly moved her to Soulaines—a demotion in influence. While wounded, Theodore made use of the new assignment by apprenticing with a doctor of Soulaines, learning nursing and pharmacy over the next six years.

Becoming medically proficient was resonant with the goals of her order. It was also personally helpful. Theodore had contracted an illness during her novitiate, possibly smallpox, which had been treated with harsh medicines causing permanent digestive damage. For the rest of her life, Theodore's diet was limited to gruel, soft foods, and a bit of squirrel broth. Constrained nourishment contributed to her frailness and susceptibility to illnesses that would be a lifelong trial.

In 1839, Theodore's life took an unexpected turn. Monsignor Celestine de La Hailandière, vicar general of the diocese of Vincennes, Indiana, on the American frontier, arrived in France commissioned to persuade sisters to emigrate. His bishop was Simon Bruté, the most learned man in America, soul friend to Elizabeth Seton, and a Breton like Theodore. The ailing Bruté had deputized his vicar general to locate teaching sisters, which brought the Monsignor to Mother Mary's door. Before De La Hailandière left France, news of Bruté's death reached him. The Monsignor had been named the next Bishop of Vincennes, quickening his mission's urgency.

Mother Mary told the Monsignor only one of her sisters had the character to lead a frontier mission: Sister Theodore. If she refused it, there would be no mission. Yet Theodore didn't submit her name for consideration. One reason was her poor health. Also, at forty-one, she was rather old for pioneering. Mother Mary informed Theodore that the entire mission rested on her; the woman who always wanted to help gave in. Five sisters were selected to make the journey with her: Vincent, Basilide, Olympiade, Xavier, and Liguori.

Monsignor De La Hailandière had procured another candidate while gathering funds around France: Irma Le Fer de La Motte, a brilliant girl with whom the new Mother Theodore was deeply taken at first meeting. Unfortunately, Irma was physically delicate and became too ill to travel at the appointed time. Mother Mary dismissed Irma's potential: she was "good for nothing but to love God."[2] Mother Theodore privately held that such talent was vital to the new community and promised Irma she could come to America later.

A sick postulant was the least of Mother Theodore's concerns. Although Mother Mary had insisted on Theodore founding the Indiana mission, the superior's coldness toward her hadn't thawed. Mother Theodore left France without receiving the superior's traditional farewell blessing. This was a keen hurt for the woman whose loyalty had been misjudged for years. Fortunately the Bishop of Le Mans, Jean-Baptiste Bouvier, was a devoted friend to Mother Theodore and remained so to the end of his life. He gave the band of missionaries his blessing before they departed for a strange new world.

A grueling 102-day journey awaited these untraveled women. They crossed an ocean to a people who spoke a language they did not know, to penetrate a wilderness they couldn't envision. Many initial promises made to these sisters were unreliable. Despite De La Hailandière's assurances, no one came to claim them from the vessel in New York.

These Frenchwomen found it difficult to make their predicament understood in English. They were also relying on a reimbursement of their expenses to journey the rest of the way to Indiana. After more than a day and night aboard ship in the harbor, the sisters were retrieved by an ambassador of the Bishop of New York. Father Felix Varela was often dispatched to assist missionaries facing confusion upon their arrival. Varela escorted them to the home of a Brooklyn widow who made it her business to welcome incoming religious. Meanwhile, Varela made inquiries on the sisters' behalf.

Mother Theodore and her sisters were stunned by New York. They had anticipated a wilderness, and found a bustling city. They attended Mass at St. Peter's on Barclay Street. The once-shabby church where Elizabeth Seton had made her profession of faith was now a grand edifice. Mother Theodore felt reassured that she was not leading her sisters into the savage place she'd imagined the New World to be.

Father Varela located the man in Philadelphia who transacted business for the Bishop of Vincennes. Mother Theodore was advised to take her sisters there, so they rode the new railway connecting New York to Philadelphia, traveling at the surprising speed of twenty miles an hour!

In Philadelphia, their contact had received no instructions about the sisters. He did, however, advance them funds to proceed to Indiana. While in the "Queen City of America," Mother Theodore's band stayed with the obliging Sisters of Charity that Seton had founded. These sisters were used to the vagaries of dealing with French clergy and sympathized with the newcomers. They took Guérin's sisters on a tour of their city, including the waterworks. Mother Theodore judged Philadelphia in many ways grander than Paris.

Eventually a priest was located to conduct the Sisters of Providence to Vincennes. They were cautioned to wear secular dress when crossing the United States; bigotry toward Catholics was unpredictable. Their guide took them first to Baltimore, to stay again with Sisters of Charity. Hearing about Elizabeth Seton's early struggles from women who'd known their foundress personally bolstered Mother Theodore's courage. She also learned about American teaching methods from these sisters. They emphasized the importance of arts in the curriculum: "No piano, no school!"[3]

Coastal cities introduced Mother Theodore's sisters to one America. As they traveled to the interior, they encountered another America: vast, spectacular, and formidable. In Cincinnati, they stayed with poorer sisters than those they had previously encountered. The pathetic cathedral of Cincinnati, too, was unlike churches at which they had marveled in New York, Philadelphia, and Baltimore.

As their journey wore on, the poverty of the mission they were embracing became appallingly evident. Fish, potatoes, and bread were presented on the table like luxuries. A priest they met in Evansville, Indiana, was so threadbare he might have been a beggar. His home, church, and school occupied the same one-room log cabin. He admitted to sleeping under trees when conducting business around his parish territory.

Trepidations grew as the sisters arrived in Vincennes. The cathedral of their new diocese was the worst of all, with broken-paned windows, a worm-eaten communion rail, and a steeple like a failed chimney. Mother Theodore's dismay was summed up in one cry: *"Mon Dieu!"* The barn in Soulaines had been a worthier structure. A peasant's home in France would not have displayed this bishop's chair.

"When one has nothing more to lose, the heart is inaccessible to fear," the new foundress confessed.[4] The road to their new home, christened Saint Mary-of-the-Woods by Bishop Bruté, was partly underwater. Their new chaplain, Father Stanislaus Buteux, accompanied them on the last leg of the journey as their carriage filled with water. It seemed inevitable that their horse would drown before they reached higher ground. Abruptly, their journey ended—in the middle of nowhere. The sisters were amazed that Father Buteux, a well-born Parisian priest of fine education, had chosen to serve in this dark forest.

The chapel intended for the sisters had recently burned down. The priest's rude cabin now doubled as the place where Mass was celebrated. There was no tabernacle. Three boards propped on stakes served for an altar. As the sisters knelt in that humble space for the first time, Mother Theodore gained a mystical appreciation of why she was here: If the Lord of the Universe could choose Bethlehem and this rustic cabin, he might also choose the unlikely foundation of Saint Mary-of-the-Woods.

Bishop De La Hailandière had misjudged the construction of the convent, and it would not be completed until the spring. The sisters were to spend the winter with the Thrall family in their farmhouse. Four postulants recruited by the bishop awaited them at the farmhouse as well. One was a former Sister of Charity who'd been persuaded by the bishop to defect to the Sisters of Providence. This violated the rule of their order: not to admit women disloyal to a prior community. Mother Theodore decided to concede to the bishop's choice. Sister

Aloysia, as she would now be known, was bilingual, a good musician, and an excellent teacher. As the French sisters had to learn English, having an in-house translator and tutor was valuable.

Mother Theodore could embrace poverty, but squeezing into another family's home was no way to establish the routines of communal life. Within a month, she convinced the bishop to help her buy the farmhouse from the Thralls. With the long journey behind them and a temporary convent secured, Mother Theodore physically collapsed.

As she would admit later in life, she was "never really well—just a little less sick."[5] From Christmas through mid-February, she endured an attack of brain fever. This malady, common in her century, sometimes meant encephalitis or other inflammations of the brain. The term also described severe mental distress that mimicked such conditions. Theodore's attack was so serious, she received the last sacraments as the bishop feared his foundress would be lost. Yet Mother Theodore rallied, as she would many times over the next sixteen years. There was still much she could do to help.

The situation that first winter was quite stark. The community had meat, cabbage, and wood: the Thralls had left a cow, some pigs, and chickens. But they were isolated by geography and language, with no schoolhouse, students, or friends. They could expect no recruits from Ruillé, and little financial support. For now they had to rely on Bishop De La Hailandière, who produced a wild card at every turn. Mother Theodore faced twin heartaches through the years: one, the cool silence of her old superior in Ruillé, who seemed determined not to support her. The other was her local bishop, whose authority became increasingly erratic.

Mother Mary of Ruillé seems to have been a person who could hold a grudge. But the modern reader of Guérin's biography cannot help but ask the question: What was going on with Bishop De La Hailandière? Medicine of the past was no exact science, and historians are loath to diagnose a problematic clergyman from a distance of two centuries. Still, the bishop could only charitably be described as suffering from mental illness. Allies and adversaries among his priests described him as "a thunderbolt," changeable in judgment, jealous for his authority, and a sad man unable to distinguish between friend and foe.

De La Hailandière himself bewailed the "sea of bitterness rising against me every way I turn."[6] The bishop could be generous and encouraging or withholding and cruel; apologetic one hour and causing more harm the next. Mother Theodore, sensitive of her bishop's reputation, kept most of what she personally thought of him off the public record. Yet the portrait emerges of a deeply wounded prelate wreaking havoc on a dependent group of women, his respect for them eroding as his terrible need to control them swelled.

The property of Saint Mary-of-the-Woods had been acquired through a gift of the Picquet family of France, members of which had emigrated to Indiana. The terms stipulated that the deed be given to the religious order serving there. Saint Mary-of-the-Woods, then, belonged to the Sisters of Providence—yet the bishop held captive both the deed and their future. Despite his often-gracious manner in the early days, the bishop did not reimburse Mother Theodore the advance money Mother Mary had put up for their sea voyage, as he had agreed to do. Into this rocky soil, the seeds of later misery were sown.

At first, deeds and dollars were not as paramount as founding a school. Public education was not widely established in the United States of the 1840s. The "common school" was just taking root in the northeast. Occasional one-room schools around the frontier lands offered the "three Rs"—reading, writing, and arithmetic—but fewer than a fifth of Indiana's 250,000 children attended.

In this context, the Sisters of Providence opened an academy for girls with a curriculum featuring reading, writing, arithmetic, geography, history (ancient and modern), composition, natural philosophy, chemistry, botany, mythology, biography, astronomy, rhetoric, plain and fancy needlework, bead work, tapestry, and lace work. With room and board, annual tuition was one hundred dollars. Extra could be paid for French, German, Latin, Italian, music, drawing, and painting. The sisters used maps, charts, and blackboards in the classroom, all typical in France but rare in the U.S.

A French education had great appeal, and Protestants flocked to enroll their daughters. Even if they didn't approve of the Catholic Church, they wanted these advantages for their children. Immigrant Catholics were too poor to afford such an education; they would have to wait for the free school to open. The first applicants were local, but by the second term students came from as far away as Pittsburgh. Mother Theodore had originally despaired that the academy seemed too inaccessible to succeed. The frontier reality was that everything is inaccessible, so distances were negotiable.

For the Sisters of Providence, 1841 was a hopeful year. Irma Le Fer de La Motte, the frail postulant left behind in France, arrived at last and received the name Francis Xavier. Her artistic talents were a great addition to the academy. Mother Theodore had learned enough English to forego an interpreter. As postulants and students multiplied, the new building was expanded, and the property provided enough food to sustain the community through the winter.

The trials began in 1842. Sr. Aloysia, defector from the Sisters of Charity, became resentful of her subordinate position at the Woods, and she allied with Father Buteaux and four postulants to start a new order. They opened a rival school in Terre Haute, spreading rumors about shocking abuses at the academy. The Sisters of Providence lost most of their paying students. Buteaux was replaced by a new chaplain, Father John Corbe, who became a wise counselor and friend to the sisters. In time, the school in Terre Haute failed, and students returned to the Woods.

The sisters opened a new mission in Jasper that same year. Jasper wasn't friendly to the Catholic presence, but the sisters overcame the suspicion of their Protestant neighbors as they always did: by offering the best education possible to their children. The sisters were surprised to learn they were expected to care for the parish priest as well as to run the school. They taught, did church linens and the priest's laundry, and cooked his meals—on top of milking their cows, doing their housework and that of the school. When Mother Theodore protested this misuse of her sisters, the bishop told her a priest was the natural superior of sisters in his parish. The bishop also asked Mother Theodore to resign as head of her order, but she resisted the recommendation.

The next mission assignment was St. Francisville, and it delivered a shock: some of the Catholic children had never heard the name of God, and older teens had not made First Communion. The worst blow came that autumn: fire destroyed the barn and harvest at the Woods. It seemed like arson, but that couldn't be proven. The loss meant destitution as winter approached. The sisters were already being denied credit by suppliers as the formerly muted anti-Catholic bias of the region was fanned into literal flames, and convent burnings were becoming common.

The Know-Nothing movement was behind the bigotry, spreading paranoia with leaflets and newspapers, creating a climate that encouraged hostility toward Catholics. The members of this secret society "covered the face of America like a flock of sparrows" in Mother Theodore's description.[7] Rumors describing treachery by the sisters would routinely wash through the district. Such prejudice affected their mission in Madison in 1844, where the sisters were mocked, spat upon, and stoned as they walked the streets.

Obstacles mounted by presumed allies were more painful still. Bishop De La Hailandière, who had once openly admired Mother Theodore, increasingly regarded her as an adversary. He forbade her to visit the missions run by her sisters; they were to be administered exclusively by local pastors. Several times when the bishop knew Theodore was away from Saint Mary-of-the-Woods, he traveled there, accepted new postulants, finalized the vows of novices, held elections for a new superior—and grew more furious each time the sisters reelected their Mother.

Theodore pondered whether the bishop's contest with her was personal, or a symptom of the devaluation of women in the United States as she had experienced it. "One does not see a woman in this country involved in the smallest business affairs," she observed. "They stare at me in Terre Haute and elsewhere when they see me doing business, paying, purchasing."[8] American women were not to wield authority of any sort: "Women in this country are as yet only one-fourth of the family. I hope through the influence of religion and education women will eventually become at least half—and the better half!"[9]

Unable to procure the deed for their property, and unwilling to expand her community's investment without it, Mother Theodore returned to France in 1843 to clarify what assistance to expect from Ruillé, and what authority to accept from Vincennes. She left fragile Sister Francis in charge of the Woods.

For much of the year she was absent, Mother Theodore also did fundraising around France as Bishop De La Hailandière had advised. Once she was out of the country, the bishop deposed Sister Francis, installed Sister Basilide, closed the St. Francisville mission, and moved the sisters there to St. Peter. He also opened a new mission in Vincennes, added new members to the community, and insisted on the election of a new superior. Finally, he made it clear that Mother Theodore was unwelcome to return to his diocese. If any sisters attempted to join their Mother in exile, they would be excommunicated.

Hysterical reports from Saint Mary-of-the-Woods reached France. Bishop Bouvier and Mother Mary advised Mother Theodore to resume her command. She was obliged to return by way of New Orleans, where a local fever immobilized her. The Ursulines nursed her until she could continue north.

Mother Theodore went directly to Vincennes to discover she had been dismissed from her order and driven from the diocese. When she faced the bishop, De La Hailandière forced the still-weakened Guérin to stand for two hours as he raved about her offenses, declared the funds she'd raised in France as theft from his diocese, and accused her of feigning illness and conspiring against him in New Orleans. He demanded a retraction of statements she hadn't made.

Mother Theodore agreed to admit any fault if the bishop would surrender the deed to Saint Mary-of-the-Woods, which rightfully belonged to her sisters. She also asked permission to exercise authority over her community according to their rule. The bishop agreed to both conditions—and later refused to do either.

During his *ad limina* visit to Rome the next year, a despairing Bishop De La Hailandière offered his resignation at age forty-six. It wasn't accepted. He returned to Vincennes bitterly, initiating another maddening cycle of promises to Mother Theodore that he would later revoke.

From Le Mans, Bishop Bouvier tried to intervene on behalf of the sisters with letters to Vincennes. Bouvier privately gave the sisters his permission to return to France or reestablish themselves elsewhere in the U.S. They didn't lack options: bishops in Detroit, New York, New Orleans, and Texas bid for the Sisters of Providence. But the sisters' investment, financial and personal, was already high in Indiana.

The crisis emerged in 1846: the sisters had to build at the Woods again to increase enrollment. But to continue to expand on property they didn't own was foolish. During another long season of negotiation and recrimination, Mother Theodore developed pneumonia.

The sisters opened a mission in Fort Wayne that same year. The Native American population was considerable in this district, and the Sisters of Providence were glad to count the children of chiefs among their students.

Despite harsh winters, cholera, and fevers frequent to the Wabash River area, the first losses to the community did not come until 1847. Sister Liguori died of cholera, followed by a postulant two weeks later. Mother Theodore herself fell ill, but insisted on making visitations to her missions. This drew a summons to the cathedral, where the bishop declared her authority illegitimate and demanded her resignation. He denied her permission to leave until she submitted, then locked her in his study and went to his dinner.

When the Vincennes sisters came looking for their superior, De La Hailandière pronounced sentence in front of them all: Guérin was no longer their Mother, nor even a sister. He released her from vows and commanded her departure from his diocese immediately and in disgrace. If the sisters attempted to follow, they were forbidden to take anything except the surety of their excommunication.

Her chronic pleurisy stirred up again, Mother Theodore was taken to the Vincennes convent where she hovered near death. The bishop sent her a confessor but withheld last rites. The sisters sent for their own chaplain, Father Corbe. When it became known at the Woods that their Mother was barred from returning, all determined to leave with her—including Corbe.

After ten days of crisis and chaos, a letter arrived from Rome: De La Hailandière's resignation had been belatedly accepted. Mother Theodore was immediately reinstated at Saint Mary-of-the-Woods. When the new bishop, John Stephen Bazin, arrived from Mobile, Alabama, he cheerfully surrendered the property deed to Mother Theodore, dismissing his predecessor's reluctance with a shrug: "Like Don Quixote he tilts against windmills."[10]

Bishop Bazin entered into a wonderful collaboration with the Sisters of Providence, but the first Indiana winter proved too much for him: He was buried at the cathedral by Easter. De La Hailandière, in retirement in Baltimore, asked for reinstatement in Vincennes and was ignored. He returned to France.

Mother Theodore's sisters opened more schools in Terre Haute, Evansville, North Madison, Lanesville, and Columbus. They ran several pharmacies and, after the cholera outbreak of 1849–1850, two orphanages in Vincennes for children of the victims. Even with the advent of public education in Indiana in 1850, 1,200 students were enrolled in Mother Theodore's schools in 1855.

Each winter Mother Theodore's fevers returned, leaving her weaker. When Sister Francis died after a short illness in 1856, her superior felt as if something essential had been lost. Whenever the burdens of her office had distracted her at prayer, Mother Theodore had looked to this sister across the chapel who was "good for nothing but to love God," and felt peace restored to her.

Two months after burying Sister Francis, Mother Theodore took to her bed for the last time. Three times in six years she had received the last sacraments, and this time they were final. Her sisters mourned their Mother for her enduring sense of humor, "her spacious mind, her admirable character, and the precious qualities of her heart."[11] Mother Theodore Guérin had added her name with a flourish to the list of those who prove what a woman can do to help.

Today

The Sisters of Providence offer literacy programs for adults, care for the sick and dying, facilitate child care, eco-justice, and nonviolence, as well as continuing their teaching mission in Taiwan, China, South America, and the West Indies. More than fifty-two hundred women have entered Mother Theodore's order. Saint Mary-of-the-Woods, founded in 1840, is the oldest Catholic women's college in the U.S. The Shrine of St. Mother Theodore Guérin, where her body lies, is located there in the Church of the Immaculate Conception.

Timeline

1790: French Revolution begins reign of terror until 1799
1798: Anne-Thérèse Guérin born at Étables, France, on October 2
1800: Indiana Territory organized; becomes a state in 1816
1823: Guérin enters Sisters of Providence at Ruillé as Sister Theodore
1826: Guérin assigned to Rennes
1834: Guérin assigned to Soulaines; Simon Bruté named first bishop of Vincennes, Indiana
1840: Guérin settles at Saint Mary-of-the-Woods
1842: First mission schools open; arson destroys the harvest
1843: Guérin goes to France to confirm her authority
1847: Bishop De La Hailandière removes and banishes Mother Theodore
1856: Mother Theodore dies at Saint Mary-of-the-Woods on May 14 at age fifty-seven

71 John Nepomucene Neumann
(1811–1860)
The Little Bishop That Could
Feast: January 5. Venerable: 1921. Beatified: 1963. Canonized: 1977.

O Lord Jesus, I believe in you, I hope in you, I love you, and I grieve of having ever offended you! Behold my resolution to live entirely for you.[1]

The canon of saints is liberally sprinkled with bishops of every age, from Augustine to Nicholas to Patrick, including forty-two Bishops of Rome, from the apostle Peter to John Paul II. The scandal-burdened beginnings of the twenty-first century United States episcopacy might make the addition of any American bishops to that list seem unlikely. But John Nepomucene Neumann, the fourth bishop of Philadelphia who served the region from 1852 until his untimely death eight years later, has earned his spot in these hallowed ranks.

Bohemia, known today as the Czech Republic, has a history of producing saints. Some names are familiar, like tenth-century "good" King Wenceslas—actually a duke, but declared a king after his death; others are not, like his granddaughter, St. Ludmilla. Another name also stands out: St. John Nepomucene, parish priest of Prague in the fourteenth century, a great preacher and confessor of the queen. Because the priest wouldn't divulge the secret of her confession to her wicked husband, King Wenceslas IV (bad King Wenceslas?), Nepomucene was thrown into the Vltava River and drowned. A bronze cross and statue mark the spot on the Charles Bridge in Prague where the saint became the first martyr of the Seal of the Confessional.

It was to honor this patron saint of Bohemia that the third child born to Philip and Agnes Neumann on Good Friday, 1811, in the remote mountain village of Prachatitz, was named. Like his namesake, John Nepomucene Neumann would make his mark as a great priest and miracle worker four thousand miles away, in the heart of the newly formed republic of the United States.

Neumann's mother was devout and pious. She attended Mass every day and received Communion frequently. She made it a practice to take one of her six young children with her to devotions. Young John, by his own account, was often reluctant to go along to Mass, the rosary, and Stations of the Cross unless the deal was sweetened by the offer of a penny. When the mother of one of his little friends complained to her son that he should be more like John, the boy replied, "Give me a penny every day and I will be just like him!"[2]

John got good marks in school but, ever humble, attributed them to his father's powerful political influence in the town. He also received from his father a love of reading. While other children played games and chased each other around, John invested his time in devouring every book he could get his hands on.

One of those books was a catechism, most likely written in German, Neumann's native language. So proficient did he become at Christian doctrine that he was confirmed at eight and received First Communion at ten, unusually early ages for that time.

Like Catholic children of every generation, John had a little altar and "played Mass." But the first real indication that he was destined for religious life came at the dinner table after the family had recited the blessing before meals. Instead of tracing the customary three crosses on his forehead, lips, and heart, Neumann reports in his autobiography that he thoughtlessly made the Sign of the Cross over the table, a gesture reserved for ecclesiastics. "See," someone exclaimed, "our little John is going to be a priest."[3] This event was recounted often by his mother and duly added to his legend.

Not that John was keen on becoming a priest; he wasn't. But, encouraged by his mother, he did study the requisite Latin under a local catechist and entered the Gymnasium at Budweis to study religion at the age of twelve. There, the courses were simply too easy for the book-learned boy. One of his professors was "given to drink," Neumann noted, and another was "dryness and dullness personified."[4]

Though discouraged, he pressed on. At eighteen he began philosophy studies and his interest began to build. He found great enjoyment in the natural sciences: physics, astronomy, biology, geology, geography and botany. By 1831 he was ready to move on to the study of medicine in Prague.

His mother was not happy. Agnes Neumann wanted her son to be a priest. Thinking he wasn't qualified, John nevertheless applied to the

Theological Seminary in Budweis (a city more famous for its beer than its seminary), mostly to make his mother happy. Much to his surprise, and maybe to his chagrin, he was accepted. Agnes was thrilled.

John took it as a sign. Maybe God was truly calling him to be a priest. It would become a family tradition, as two of his sisters and a brother entered religious orders. So he entered seminary in 1831, plunging into his studies with renewed vigor, determined to be the best priest he could be.

It was in Budweis that he was caught the missionary fever. Reports poured in from missionary priests serving the German-speaking communities of North America, and Neumann wanted to be part of this. He turned his wholehearted attention to acquiring the skills necessary for the missions. He wrangled a scholarship to the University of Prague to study French and English, requisite languages for work in the European diaspora living in the U.S. It was not that Neumann's native German would be of little use there; by the end of the nineteenth century, German-speaking immigrants accounted for roughly one-sixth of all American Catholics. Next to the Irish and Italians, Germans contributed the most Catholics to the American population.

Complex factors fueled the mass movement to America. The industrial revolution was in full swing in Europe. The steam engine, perfected only a few decades earlier, had migrated from factories to transportation. Travel to seaports was safer, faster, and cheaper than ever before. Steamships made the passage to America more inviting. The death of Jean Lafitte in 1823 spelled the end of the Golden Age of Piracy, so seagoing travelers had a much better chance of arriving at their destinations with their lives and belongings intact.

Meanwhile, disease and famine remained a threat in central Europe. A cholera epidemic raged through Germany in 1830. Crop failure, soaring food prices, and widespread hunger characterized the 1840s. Political unrest and conflict between warring factions of the German Confederation signaled for many that it was time to go, and America, so they were hearing, was the place.

Young seminarian Neumann was ready to join the tide of emigration headed for the Land of Opportunity, but fate threw some roadblocks in his way. First the bishop, fearing that diocesan resources were being invested in men headed elsewhere, decided seminarians shouldn't take language classes. Next, money distinctly pledged to aid a priest-candidate from Bohemia in traveling to the U.S. was given to another missionary—from Alsace-Lorraine. Finally, when Neumann completed his studies and applied for ordination in 1835, the bishop cited an overabundance of clerics in Bohemia and determined no priests would be ordained that year.

These events might have derailed anyone's plans. But Neumann, driven by the conviction that he was called to priesthood and to the American missions, pressed on. He applied to the Bishop of Philadelphia but, with an irony perceptible only to history, was denied. He next wrote to Simon Bruté, Bishop of the Diocese of Vincennes in Indiana.

Without waiting for a reply, he set about getting himself to America. He scrounged up money. He begged accommodations from friends and friends of friends. He finagled transportation, at one point trudging through the night in the rain; at another, by his own account, traversing the 150 miles from Paris to Le Havre on the roof of a stagecoach "behind the driver's seat and sitting next to a Jew."[5] Arriving at the port in Le Havre, he discovered Bishop Bruté had accepted the application of another—and not his.

Faith is more than just an intellectual assent to the existence of God. Faith also means trust. At this point in his odyssey, Neumann had to trust in God. He was totally on his own. Without any assurance of what awaited him across the ocean, he purchased passage for New York. He spread his possessions—two bags, a box of books, a straw mattress, a sack of potatoes, some biscuits, a ham, and a cooking pot—on a small patch of deck amidships and settled in for the seven-week voyage to his destiny.

Contrary winds, bouts of seasickness, and a near miss when a topmast came crashing down in a raging storm marked his passage. On Trinity

Sunday, 1835, Neumann arrived in New York. He presented himself, hat in hand, to John Dubois, Bishop of New York, who put him to work teaching German-speaking children of the city.

Decades earlier, Dubois had founded Mount St. Mary's College in Emmitsburg, Maryland. It was with his support that Elizabeth Seton established the first U.S. congregation of religious sisters at Emmitsburg, inaugurating the Catholic parochial school system in America. Now, almost thirty years later, Bishop Dubois ordained another American saint, John Nepomucene Neumann, at what is now Old St. Patrick's Cathedral in New York City. The diminutive Neumann must not have made much of an impression on Dubois; at five feet two, he was hardly an imposing figure. Thereafter, Dubois referred to Neumann as "that little priest, Father What's-his-name."[6]

Then, as now, the new recruit gets the most difficult assignments. Bishop Dubois promptly sent Father Neumann to the far reaches of upstate New York, to a stretch of land between Lake Ontario and Lake Erie known as the Niagara Region, near the newly incorporated city of Buffalo at the western end of the Erie Canal. Throngs of Irish and German Catholics were flocking there to take advantage of the economic boom generated by the canal and the extension of the railroads. Neumann's job was to pastor this wild bunch of immigrants and establish a united Catholic presence in the region.

The task wasn't easy. Largely working class and uneducated, these Catholics held widely disparate customs and religious practices. The Germans were antagonistic toward the Irish, and the Irish toward the Germans. Neither looked kindly on the French Canadians coming across the nearby border looking for work. Mixed in were the local band of Tonawanda, creating a toxic brew of intolerance and bigotry. Pastoring them all was like herding cats.

Adding to the difficulties was the social climate of nineteenth-century America, which was decidedly anti-Catholic. Sixty years earlier, the nation had been established by throwing off the shackles of foreign domination. Civil liberty and religious freedom were the hallmarks of this new republic, and second-generation Americans were suspicious of foreigners, especially Catholics. For many, religious freedom meant freedom from the "Romanish religion" ruled by an Italian dictator. Attempts were made by state legislative bodies in New York to curtail immigration from "Catholic" countries such as Ireland, Italy, and Germany, and to restrict their civil rights. *Awful Disclosures of Maria Monk*, an 1836 novel purporting to reveal lurid details of life in a Canadian convent—complete with debauching priests, a secret tunnel between rectory and nunnery, and smothered newborns—was a best-seller of the period.

Samuel Morse, after whom Morse Code is named and who held patents for the electronic telegraph, was a prolific author of anti-Catholic editorials and tracts. In 1835 he asserted in *The New York Observer* that Catholic immigration to the United States was a vast Vatican conspiracy to take over the country. Colonies of Italian, Irish, and German Catholics, Morse claimed, were being strategically placed throughout New York, New England, the Great Lakes, and the Mississippi Valley in order to rise up at a secret signal and establish Roman rule in the states. The whole scheme, he alleged, was run by the Jesuits. Morse called for American Protestants to unite against the Catholic menace, declaring that "Popery is now, what it has ever been, a system of the darkest *political intrigue and despotism,* cloaking itself to avoid attack under the sacred name of religion."[7]

From this vehement anti-Catholic undercurrent came the Know-Nothing movement, a secret society of nativists that rose to brief prominence in the mid-1800s. By the 1850s over a million U.S. voters had signed up with the movement's political wing, the American Party. Its most prominent member was the former Whig, Millard Fillmore, the thirteenth president of the United States.

As if this all weren't enough, the sheer geography of Neumann's responsibilities was staggering. The first year he pastored three parishes in the Niagara region: Williamsville, ten miles north of Buffalo; Lancaster, eight miles to the south; and North Bush, now the town of Tonawanda, ten miles northwest. Additionally, he regularly visited two small, German-speaking communities, fifty miles away on the south shore of Lake Ontario and thirty miles east in Batavia. He also taught school for six months at the church in Williamsville because they couldn't afford a teacher. Neumann couldn't come up with room and board in Williamsville, so he moved in with a friendly farmer in North Bush, a mile and a half away from his church—through the marshy woods on foot.

In 1837 a parish in Rochester, a day's journey to the east, was added to his load. A priest was sent to take the parishes in Williamsville and Lancaster, but he turned out to be more of a burden than a help, and after a few weeks was sent back. The next year Sheldon, another parish thirty miles to the southeast, was added to Neumann's growing list of responsibilities.

Neumann struggled in this assignment. He met resistance from nativist locals who didn't particularly like the little foreign priest who couldn't speak English. Trustees of the parishes gave him a hard time, too, and often challenged his authority. Neumann wasn't much of an authoritarian, so he met their hostility with kindness and courtesy.

While his gentleness proved to be fairly effective in dealing with human problems, it failed to impress his horse. Loath to use spur or whip on the animal, Neumann tried to influence its gait and direction with kind words and polite gestures. The horse, for its part, had a mind of its own and often followed whim and fancy, carrying Neumann miles from his intended destination. One problem seemed to be that, despite maximum adjustment, Neumann's legs weren't long enough to reach the stirrups. His total lack of horsemanship was another problem. One story has it that he occasionally mounted with the wrong foot and found himself facing backwards in the saddle. He eventually gave up on the nag and made his rounds on foot, sometimes slogging twenty miles or more through the woods.

One winter night Neumann was found lying unconscious in the muck by a party of Tonawanda, who tended to him and carried him to safety. The Know-Nothings also caused a great deal of trouble. After a particularly nasty public debate, a band of masked men accosted him in the woods on his way home and threatened him with a noose. Again the Tonawanda came to his rescue. Ironically, this band of the Seneca were members of the same Iroquois Confederacy as the Mohawk who put to death the Jesuit martyrs two hundred years before, yet they twice saved this nineteenth-century priest from death.

Finally, after four years in an impossible job, the work caught up with Neumann and he took sick with a fever for three months in the spring of 1840. While recuperating in the Rochester rectory, he considered a change. His movements around western New York had brought him into contact with priests of the Congregation of the Most Holy Redeemer. Their piety and zeal, and the good these Redemptorists had accomplished, impressed Neumann. He saw the value of living in a community of priests where, in his words, "I would not have to be exposed alone to the thousand dangers of the world."[8] He requested entrance into the order and was accepted later that fall.

A month later Neumann arrived at the Redemptorist parish in Pittsburgh, delighted to be free from the crushing weight of his responsibilities in New York. Little did he know even greater burdens were on the way.

While in Pittsburgh, the Redemptorist superior Father Prost arrived to receive Neumann's vows and to invest him with the habit of the order. Unfortunately, Prost had forgotten to bring his ritual book and had to compose the rite from memory. Despite the unusual nature of the ceremony, in November of 1840, Neumann became the first priest in the U.S. to join the Redemptorists.

Like the ceremony of his investiture, Neumann had to invent his own novitiate since there was no formal Redemptorist novitiate operating in the country. He followed his order's rule meticulously, filling the hours of the day with meditations, visits to the Blessed Sacrament, examinations of conscience, spiritual readings, and recitation of the rosary—and made sure everybody else in the house did so as well.

Six months later, in an attempt to provide Father Neumann with a real novitiate, the Redemptorists sent him to their house in Baltimore. Upon his arrival he found there was no room for him in the small house filled with a dozen priests and brothers. They sent him on an eight-month odyssey through New York, Pennsylvania, Ohio, and West Virginia, where he helped out in a wide variety of pastoral settings before returning to Baltimore. Even there, lacking proper books and directives from Europe, Neumann's novitiate was cobbled together as best they could and as far as they knew. In spite of the difficulties, Neumann made his final vows in January of 1842 at St. James the Less Church in Baltimore.

Preaching was the mainstay of the Redemptorist mission: proclaiming the Word through parish missions, retreats, and other forms of spiritual teaching. Most importantly for Neumann, they followed a rule and lived in community. "The important thing, Father, is that we be docile to orders," the Redemptorists taught Neumann. "If we obey, we're doing God's will."[9]

The newly professed Neumann settled into life at the Redemptorist house in Baltimore. He loved it. In his journal he notes these were the happiest years of his life. As a lowly curate, not a superior, he had few administrative responsibilities. He got to do the things he was good at: praying, studying, preaching, teaching, and caring for the thousands of German-speaking immigrant families arriving in Baltimore every day. Maryland was a haven for Catholics, and Baltimore was the first episcopal see in the United States. Compared to the hostile environs of Buffalo, Neumann was in Catholic heaven.

This happy state didn't last long. In early 1844, less than two years after his profession, he was sent to Pittsburgh to become the superior of St. Philomena's, a Redemptorist church in the heart of the city. The trouble was that there was no church. Neumann had to build it.

This was Neumann's worst nightmare. All he wanted to do was to be a good priest. Nothing in his seminary training, religious formation, or previous assignments had prepared him for this. What did he know about building a church? His only consolation was reliance on the Redemptorist rule and community. His hopeless administrative skills would not build this church, but his prayers could. It quickly became known at St. Philomena's that if you needed Father Superior, look no further than the chapel.

The consolation Neumann found in living with like-minded priests and brothers took a considerable upswing with the arrival of a newly ordained Redemptorist priest from Bavaria, Francis Xavier Seelos. Neumann and Father Franz hit it off right away. Their zeal and piety meshed wonderfully. They saw eye-to-eye on just about everything—except for their disparate height. The short, stocky Neumann and tall, slender Seelos standing together on the sidewalk looked like a fireplug next to a lamppost.

The two priests teamed up on missions and retreats in the city and outlying communities. They taught, preached, and cared for the poor, the sick, and the dying, all the while managing to build the biggest church thus far in the city of Pittsburgh. Seelos acknowledged the guidance of his superior as confessor and spiritual director. The two men were considered saints by the people they served. Neumann, ever humble, even shared his room with Seelos, hanging a blanket to divide the two sides.

Three years after arriving at St. Philomena's, once again hard work caught up with Neumann and he became terribly ill. After months of fever and bronchitis, in 1847 he was recalled to Baltimore, leaving the unfinished church behind.

Warmed by the Chesapeake, Baltimore's climate was a balm for Neumann and soon he was well again, happily taking up his duties as a simple parish priest. The relief and joy of this freedom from responsibility was short-lived. Within a month, a letter arrived from the Redemptorist superior in Belgium naming Neumann as the order's new provincial in America. The young priest, only five years professed, now had command and responsibility for all priests and brothers living in ten Redemptorist houses and seventy mission outposts in the United States. He was horrified, but he couldn't say no. He was bound by obedience, which assured him he was doing God's will.

Others didn't think so. The appointment won Neumann more critics than allies. Many of his confreres, longer-serving in more difficult positions, had been passed over for the job and they were not happy about it. Some protested that he had never completed a real novitiate. Others questioned the validity of his ad-libbed investiture. Still others questioned his stature, both among the Redemptorists and measured with a yardstick. Men in his house complained of being treated like novices, as Neumann insisted on punctual compliance with the rule. Others just didn't like him. But the people of St. Alphonsus Church, where he lived and worked, loved him. They declared the little priest a living saint.

Two years of division and squabbling among the Redemptorists were enough for Neumann. He petitioned his European superiors to be relieved of his duties, and in 1849 his replacement arrived. Reduced to being a simple priest again, Neumann heaved a great sigh of relief and breathed in the sweet air of freedom.

Like all of Neumann's forays into the simple life, this one did not last long. During the winter of 1851–1852, rumors began to swirl in Baltimore that he was going to be made a bishop. Neumann, frightened out of his wits by the scuttlebutt, ran to all the various convents in town where he was spiritual director. "Make a novena!" he implored the sisters. "Make many novenas!" "For what intention, Father?" they asked. "To avert impending harm to the Church in America!" he replied.[10]

Despite the novenas, John Neumann was named the fourth Bishop of Philadelphia in 1852 by Pope Pius IX and consecrated that March on his forty-first birthday. The see of Philadelphia was enormous. Spread over thirty-five thousand square miles, it comprised eastern Pennsylvania, the southern half of New Jersey, and all of Delaware. There were ninety-two churches, over a hundred priests, five colleges, a seminary, a hospital, and numerous other religious institutions. Having mainly served German-speaking communities so far, Neumann had gotten by with a modicum of English. He had become fairly fluent in Spanish, Gaelic, and Italian. Now he would have to learn the difficult language of American English in earnest.

Factions in Philadelphia didn't approve of a foreign bishop who didn't speak much English. The nativists looked on Neumann with suspicion and hostility. The Know-Nothings mounted a malicious campaign against him. They portrayed him in leaflets as a sure sign of the papal plot to seize the country. They called him "a meddlesome foreigner," "a lackey of the greedy, autocratic schemers in Rome," and "a sworn enemy of American institutions."[11]

There were real threats of danger in these calumnies. Only eight years before, Philadelphia had been the scene of the 1844 Nativist Riots, ignited when Bishop Francis Patrick Kenrick, Neumann's predecessor, requested that Catholic children in public schools be allowed to read from Catholic Douay-Rheims Bibles instead of the Protestant Bibles in standard use. Enraged by reports that the bishop was trying to ban the Bible from public schools, a mob of Protestant nativists attacked and burned St. Michael's Church and rectory, along with a convent of the Sisters of Charity in the city.

Despite Kenrick's plea for nonviolence, Catholics armed themselves to fight off the rioters. Bloody skirmishes left many churches damaged. One force of nativists, armed with muskets and cannon, advanced on St. Philip Neri Church but were repelled by a military unit of the city guard. Reinforced, the nativists tried again. This time they were met by state militia called out by the governor. The ensuing battle left fifteen dead and fifty wounded, and the church heavily damaged by cannon fire.

After the riots, unwilling to press the fight against the public schools, Bishop Kenrick encouraged the establishment of Catholic schools in the diocese instead. This is where Neumann came in. The little bishop had no desire to roll out heavy artillery against the nativists, but he did know the source of his real firepower. Armed with his rosary, he took to his chapel and stormed heaven with prayer. He invested himself totally in his duties, traveling to far-flung parishes and missions, preaching, teaching, and confirming.

In one six-week period he confirmed three thousand children. Once he trudged fifteen miles over the rugged Allegheny ridges to confer the sacrament on one child. He visited the sick. He installed lay leaders in communities where there was no church or priest. He spent hours hearing confessions in English, German, Italian, and Gaelic. "Thanks be to God we've got an Irish bishop," one woman announced, coming forth from his confessional.[12]

Neumann worked to build schools in every parish, establishing the first diocesan school system in America. He founded a religious congregation of women, the Sisters of St. Francis of Philadelphia. He built eighty new churches and two hundred schools in his diocese. Student enrollment grew from five hundred to five thousand. He increased the number of seminarians from thirty-six to fifty-eight.

In 1853 he began the Forty Hours devotion in the diocese—not just occasionally but continuously—on a rotating schedule from parish to parish, starting symbolically at St. Philip Neri, where the need to sanctify the city was great.

Neumann traveled to Rome in 1854 for the solemn pronouncement of the dogma of the Immaculate Conception of the Blessed Virgin Mary. On December 8, from among the 53 cardinals and 140 bishops gathered for the liturgy in St. Peter's Basilica, Neumann was chosen to hold the text from which Pope Pius IX would read. Shy and unassuming, Neumann was put off by the selection until he realized that *Pio Nono*, a man of small stature like himself, stood the best chance of being seen above the diminutive bishop.

Throughout his reign as Bishop of Philadelphia, Neumann worked behind the scenes to get himself extracted from the job. He recommended that a second diocese be formed in Pottsville in the state's coal region, and indicated he'd be happy to take the humbler job. That didn't work. When it was suggested that North Carolina be made a diocese, Neumann offered to take that job, but was again refused. Like it or not, he would remain Bishop of Philadelphia until his dying day.

That day came on January 5, 1860. Neumann was returning to his home down Vine Street around three o'clock in the afternoon when something vital inside the man broke down. He collapsed on the stoop of the Quayne house and was carried inside by passersby. In a few moments he was gone, free once and for all from the job he never wanted. He was forty-eight.

Neumann's life was a marathon of end-on-end experiences of the divine mystery, of curious intersections that were more than coincidences, of events flowing resolutely in one direction toward a holy purpose. He set his heart toward that purpose and lived convinced that the world around him would comply by arranging resources, people, and grace to accomplish what he set out to do. And because this little man believed so fiercely, even the stoop where he died became a source of healing and hope for many.

Today

The Redemptorists, now 5,500 strong, serve in foreign missions in 77 countries around the world. In addition to Neumann, three other Redemptorists have been canonized, including their founder, Alphonsus Liguori. Blessed Francis Xavier Seelos, who served with Neumann in Pittsburgh, is also being considered for sainthood. The miracle stoop, the marble doorstep upon which Neumann collapsed, can be seen at the National Shrine of St. John Neumann in Philadelphia. The shrine also contains the body of the saint, encased in a glass box under the altar in the lower sanctuary. In Baltimore, Neumann's room and artifacts can be viewed at his former parish, St. Alphonsus Church.

Timeline

1811: John Nepomucene Neumann born in Prachatitz, Bohemia, on March 28

1830: *The Protestant*, an anti-Catholic weekly, begins U.S. nativist movement

1836: Neumann ordained a priest for the Diocese of New York

1842: Neumann joins the Redemptorists

1847: Neumann appointed provincial of American Redemptorists

1848: Neumann becomes an American citizen; diplomatic relations established between U.S. and Papal States

1850: Holy See establishes three archbishops in Cincinnati, New Orleans, and New York

1852: Neumann consecrated fourth Bishop of Philadelphia; First Plenary Council of Baltimore
1854: Dogma of the Immaculate Conception proclaimed in Rome
1860: Neumann dies on a Philadelphia street on January 5 at age forty-eight

8] **Blessed Francis Xavier Seelos**
(1819–1867)
The Happy Healer
Feast: October 5. Venerable: 2000. Beatified: 2000.

 A long experience has taught me the great lesson that God leads men in a human manner by other men whom he appointed to be in His place and who should be of the same kindness as he himself was while on earth.[1]

A whim had brought them to the weathered old church. Vacationing in New Orleans a few years after Hurricane Katrina, Andrew and Laura were poking around the historic sites. Neither had heard of Francis Xavier Seelos, the beatified Redemptorist whose name was over the gate and whose shrine was attached to this Baroque Revival structure. Andrew stopped to read a plaque detailing the history of the church, known as St. Mary's Assumption. Then he glanced up to see Laura walking across the sanctuary with a good-sized crucifix held tightly against her arm.

Laura's arm had been a problem for a while. Some winters ago she had slipped and fallen on the ice, injuring her elbow, and had been in constant pain ever since. Having lost all but a little range of motion in the arm, she had to rely on help to accomplish the simplest daily tasks. X-rays revealed nothing and doctors had no explanation. All she could do was take pain killers and guard the damaged arm.

Jack, the docent at the Seelos shrine, had asked Laura if she suffered from any afflictions. "Oh, yeah," she replied. "My arm gives me a lot of pain. Did you ever try to wash your hair with one hand?" Jack presented her with the crucifix, explaining that it was one of Seelos's own mission crosses. It contained a first-class relic of the saint: a bone chip imbedded at its center. Relic comes from the Latin word *relinquo*, which means "I leave." What saints leave behind is precious to the Church. The mission cross itself, used by the saint personally, was considered a second-class relic. Jack instructed Laura to hold it against her damaged elbow. "It's worked for a lot of people," he told her. Laura held the crucifix against her arm for the entire tour of the church and shrine.

Later, the couple was sampling the cuisine at a restaurant in the French Quarter when Laura felt a burning sensation in her arm.

For women of a certain age, sudden powerful surges of heat are not uncommon. She dismissed it as a manifestation of menopause, but it persisted.

That night in their hotel room, Laura woke from sleep. She was used to being awakened by pain and would carefully change position to take pressure off the arm. But this night was strangely different. There was no pain. Laura flexed her arm and explored the elbow with her fingers. Nothing. A thrill ran through her body. She wanted to wake her husband at once, but confessing her suspicion embarrassed her. Better to wait until morning and see how she felt then. She was, after all, a reasonable person: religious to a degree, but not a pious hysteric.

The next morning Laura rose, anticipating the familiar little stabs that accompanied every movement. Nothing! She showered, washed her hair with both hands, dressed herself, all without pain for the first time in years. Over breakfast she confided in her husband. He was astonished. They both marveled. Had Laura been healed by the obscure saint at the shrine? What other explanation was there? Was it a miracle?

If so, it wouldn't be the first. Other pilgrims to the shrine at St. Mary's Assumption have experienced restoration through the intercession of Blessed Francis Xavier Seelos. So far only one, the healing of Angela Boudreaux in 1966, counts toward the cause of his sanctification. Angela, a New Orleans wife and mother of four small children, had lost 90 percent of her liver to a malignant tumor. Doctors told her she had weeks to live. Returning from the hospital, she stopped at Seelos's tomb to pray. She was blessed with the same mission cross Laura would later hold to her arm. Months later, Angela was still alive and the swelling in her abdomen had subsided. Subsequent gall bladder surgery years later revealed only minor scars on her liver. Angela had recovered completely.

In 2000, Angela's cure was approved by the Vatican Congregation for the Causes of Saints, and she herself was in Rome later that year for the beatification of Seelos by Pope John Paul II. One more miracle cure would launch him into sainthood. Scores of accounts have been logged, but as in Laura's healing, they were of the sort hard to document and authenticate. Then in 2004, the case of Mary Ellen Heibel surfaced. She had been diagnosed with esophageal cancer that had metastasized to her liver and lungs. Doctors had no hope of her survival and sent her home to die.

Mary Ellen still had one card to play. She was a parishioner of St. Mary's Church in Annapolis, Maryland, where Francis Seelos had served as rector one hundred and forty years earlier. Parishioners there started a novena: nine days of prayer asking for Seelos to intercede on behalf of Mary Ellen. A subsequent examination found her cancer-free.

Unfortunately, this miracle was deemed unacceptable. Mary Ellen's case was disqualified for use in the saint's cause by the tyranny of the clock. In order for a miraculous cancer cure to be authenticated by the Church, the individual must remain cancer-free for ten years. Mary Ellen didn't live that long. In 2009, she died of a lung infection, unrelated to the cancer, at age seventy-one. Seelos's sainthood continues to await the kind of miracle that can be authenticated by the book.

Heroic virtue is easier to prove. This is the quality of personal holiness that sets the sainthood process in motion for most candidates, and Seelos possessed it in volume. Everywhere he served in his priestly ministry, from Baltimore to Pittsburgh, from Detroit to New Orleans, folks who encountered him would attest: "That man is a saint."

The journey of this gifted life began on January 11, 1819, in Füssen, Germany, in the foothills of the Bavarian Alps near the Austrian border. Francis was the sixth of twelve children born to Frances Schwarzenbach and her husband, Mang Seelos. They were a devout family, and Francis absorbed this trait early from his mother, who read to him from pious books. Once, after hearing the story of Jesuit missionary Francis Xavier, young Seelos remarked, "I will be a Francis Xavier."[2]

When he could read for himself, Seelos enjoyed sharing those same pious stories with his family. His sister claimed that once Francis stumbled over the name of St. Polycarp and it came out "Polycrap." This drew great laughter from his siblings and a stern correction from his father.

Francis was an altar boy in his local parish and, as seems to be de rigueur with boys-who-become-priests, he conducted daily "Mass" for neighborhood kids on a little altar he set up at home. When his father took a job at the church and moved the family into the sacristan's house, church became an even greater part of young Seelos's life.

At age thirteen Francis entered St. Stephen's Institute at Augsburg. Ironically, this city was the site of the famous 1530 Augsburg Confession—history's first official profession of Protestant faith. His family was poor, so he could afford only one meal a day, not easy for a growing teen. His father would send a little money, but Francis would usually give it to the poorer boys so that they could eat, too. The other boys, grateful for his generosity, nicknamed him "Banker Seelos."

At Sunday Mass, Francis played the violin and accompanied the choir, but was often faulted for playing the wrong notes. The same was true of his singing, and eventually the choirmaster invited him to find other ways to assist at the liturgy. Despite such criticism, Francis maintained his cheerfulness, a trait he cultivated for a lifetime.

In the fall of 1839, Seelos took up philosophy at the Ludwig Maximilian University at Munich. He also studied dancing and fencing, belying any notion that the pious Seelos was a prig. On the contrary, he easily dissolved into laughter, which got him into trouble in those corners of religion where humor is not appreciated.

Francis did well in his studies, being consistently near the top of his class. But three years into his stay at the university, he had a mystical experience that changed the course of his life. The Blessed Virgin Mary appeared to him in a dream and indicated that he was not to remain in Germany. From that time on, Francis was bent on becoming a missionary. In 1842 he applied for admission to the Society of the Most Holy Redeemer in America.

Intercontinental communications being what they were, a reply from the U.S. was not soon forthcoming. By the summer of that year, obliged to move forward toward ordination, Seelos applied to the diocesan seminary and was accepted. Two weeks after classes began, the letter came from America; it had taken four months to arrive, but the

Redemptorists had accepted his application. He was going to be a missionary in America.

The American church was desperate for clergy to care for the thousands of immigrants arriving daily on its shores. There were as yet few homegrown vocations; seminaries were a rarity in the U.S. Priests and religious had to be recruited from Europe. The Redemptorist provincial in Baltimore pleaded for German-speaking priests to come: "If German clerics really knew the abandoned spiritual condition of Germans in the United States, and the danger they face of losing their souls, many would certainly go to their rescue."[3]

After obtaining the necessary permissions, Seelos moved out of the diocesan seminary and into the Redemptorist house in Augsburg. Life in a religious house would not be the same as it was in the seminary. His first night there, Seelos left his muddy shoes in the hall outside his room for the porter to clean and polish. The next morning they were still there, mud and all, mute testimony of things to come.

The following spring, Seelos boarded the *Saint Nicolas* out of Le Havre, bound for New York. During the passage, the missionaries accompanying Seelos avoided contact with the French laborers traveling in steerage. The ecclesiastics' delicate sensibilities were offended by their coarse language and irreligious behavior—but not Seelos. He went among the laborers and, using the French he had learned at the university, instructed them in the Gospel and taught them to pray.

Landing in New York, Seelos stayed with Redemptorists there only a few days and then headed for the community's novitiate in Baltimore. He was invested with the habit of the order, and his one-year novitiate passed routinely but fruitfully.

Seelos, it appears, used snuff. He wrote to his family that he "relished" the snuffing tobacco he got in the U.S. When instructed by his novice master to abstain from the habit, however, he gave it up readily and reported later that he hadn't taken a pinch in over a year. It was a lesson in self-denial which offered him a new moral compass: "With the grace of God from now on I will not consult my likes and dislikes and natural inclinations but only the law of the love of God and His Holy Will."[4]

His novitiate completed, Seelos took vows as a Redemptorist in 1844, and was ordained at St. James the Less Church in Baltimore. The following year he was assigned to St. Philomena's in Pittsburgh, where the rector was Father John Neumann—America's future sainted Redemptorist. The two teamed up on missions and worked very effectively together. They presented an amusing mismatched appearance, yet both were clearly saints to many who encountered them.

The two shared a meager room in the dilapidated rectory. One night during a storm, rain poured in through the leaky roof and they had to abandon the house. They wound up sleeping on benches in a local hotel lobby.

Neumann became the Redemptorist provincial in 1847 and was obliged to move to Baltimore. One of the first things he did as provincial was relocate the novitiate to the new rectory he'd left behind in Pittsburgh, and named Seelos as novice master.

Seelos discharged his duties to mixed reviews. He taught the novices well in terms of the rule and ascetical practices, but he was not evaluated as a strong leader or an effective disciplinarian. Remembering the "muddy shoe" incident of his first stay in a Redemptorist house, Seelos had the novices leave their shoes outside their rooms at night. He himself would clean and polish them, returning them before morning. Humble acts like these endeared him to his charges, but earned reproaches from his confreres.

Being novice master didn't excuse Seelos from the duties of a parish priest. In the two years he ran the novitiate, he also performed 150 marriages and 370 baptisms. Despite his difficulty with English, he was considered a good preacher, earning respect from parishioners who appreciated his efforts to communicate in their language. He visited the sick, tended to the dying, and taught the children. He also received an education in the hostility against Catholics and immigrants prevalent in nineteenth-century America.

The Know-Nothings were active in the city. One vehemently anti-Catholic Pittsburgh nativist was Joseph Barker, an illiterate street preacher. In 1849, during a particularly nasty sidewalk tirade against

Catholics, Barker was arrested for using lewd and indecent language in public. He was fined and tossed in jail. From his cell, Barker mounted a campaign to run for mayor of the city and, remarkably, won the election.

On the day of his inauguration, Barker was released temporarily under guard so he could be sworn into office. Eventually the governor pardoned Barker so that he could discharge his duties as mayor. The Redemptorists at St. Philomena's, anticipating trouble with Barker in office, hatched a plan. They turned over ownership of the church and rectory to the city, thereby forcing the mayor to protect rather than attempt to destroy what was now effectively city property.

Violent attacks and suspicious fires in churches, convents, schools, and rectories were not unknown in Pittsburgh. Seelos wrote back home to Bavaria that he was not enamored of the coarse language, love of money, and careless way of life followed by many Americans. He wasn't crazy about the insect population of the Three Rivers area, either. "If I had followed my natural inclinations," he wrote, "I never would have come here."[5]

Still Seelos, true to his nature, remained cheerful. He was known to play tricks on the other priests in the rectory; one such deception involved a new arrival. On the first morning, the newcomer came to breakfast complaining that his saliva had turned black. Pittsburgh was an industrial city thick with soot from coal-fired factories; one got used to things like black saliva in the morning. But Seelos convinced the newcomer he had contracted the notorious "Pittsburgh Crud" and would shortly die. The man's horror evoked fits of laughter from the others at table, and the prank was revealed.

Just as his friend Neumann didn't last long as provincial of the Redemptorists in Baltimore, neither did Seelos endure as novice master. A new provincial moved the novitiate back to Baltimore and Seelos became a simple parish priest again, which he loved. In 1851, Francis was made pastor of St. Philomena's. He promptly built a wall around the church and rectory to protect the property from the Know-Nothings. During the three years of his pastorate he also built an orphanage. The parish grew under his leadership, and he was revered as a preacher, confessor, and teacher. During this time, too, the power of healing began to be exhibited in this priest.

A man on crutches approached Father Seelos in the church and asked the priest to heal him; Seelos told him he didn't have the power to do that. The man evidently thought differently and threw his crutches out the window. Seelos, amazed, gave the man his blessing and the man walked from the church without any assistance. On another occasion, a woman brought her epileptic daughter to him. Seelos carried the girl to Our Lady's altar and prayed over her, then gave her back to her mother, instructing the woman to send the girl to school. The fearful mother kept the girl home and the seizures continued. She returned to Seelos and once more he prayed over the child, again ordering the mother to send the girl to school. This time she did, and the seizures never returned.

In the nine years Francis Seelos spent in Pittsburgh, he went from being a newly ordained priest, untried in pastoral work, to a legend renowned for his skill and sanctity. His parishioners without qualification called him a living saint. However, in 1854, Seelos was moved to Baltimore to become rector of St. Alphonsus parish.

St. Alphonsus was the church in Baltimore for German nationals. It had absorbed two other city parishes, St. James and St. Michael. Even with seven priests working for him, spread out over old parish boundaries and ethnic and racial lines, the work was arduous for the new pastor. Adding to his difficulties, the other priests didn't appreciate Seelos's style. They complained to the provincial that he wasn't a good leader: too kind, gentle, compassionate, merciful, and lenient. They wanted a stern authoritarian at the helm, like the ones in Europe, which Seelos was not. Even Isaac Hecker, a Redemptorist who would one day become the founder of his own religious order, the Paulists, wrote that Seelos was "most wretchedly weak."[6]

From colonial days, the city of Baltimore and the state of Maryland had been associated with the Catholic Church. Baltimore was America's first episcopal see and John Carroll the first bishop. Maryland had been a refuge for Catholics facing prejudice and restriction of civil liberties in other states. But more recent political and economic struggles, along with the constant flow of European immigrants, turned the hearts of Baltimore's population. By the 1850s the Know-Nothings were competing for the minds and votes of the people.

Two years after Seelos arrived at St. Alphonsus, riots broke out between the city's factions. Some people were killed and many injured. "If this goes on," Seelos said, "I might even have the privilege of being a martyr!"[7] That same year a Know-Nothing candidate was elected mayor of Baltimore. During the presidential election in 1856, the Know-Nothing-backed candidate Millard Fillmore won Maryland, but lost the rest of the thirty-one states to his opponents, John C. Frémont and the winner, James Buchanan.

Seelos took on the stressful environment to the detriment of his health. In late winter of 1857, he suffered a ruptured blood vessel in his throat which hemorrhaged for days. It nearly killed him. Counseled by doctors, the Redemptorist provincial pulled him out of Baltimore and sent him to Annapolis, where he would once again be a novice master. Seelos was elated and termed his brush with death a "happy sickness." But the reprieve didn't last long.

Within months, the provincial reassigned Seelos to Cumberland, Maryland, to be pastor of Saints Peter and Paul Parish as well as prefect of students at the Redemptorist seminary. He remained there for five years.

Cumberland is situated in the thin part of the Maryland panhandle: five miles of real estate between the Pennsylvania and Virginia (now West Virginia) borders, just over halfway from Baltimore to Pittsburgh. Its position on the north bank of the Potomac, at the terminus of the Chesapeake and Ohio Canal, and its proximity to the Cumberland Narrows with railroad access to the Ohio River, made it an important economic and strategic location. These factors came into play at the outbreak of the Civil War.

Seelos's tenure as prefect at the seminary ran the same course as his stint with the novices. His students loved him. He avoided the authoritative approach and chose to lead by example, encouragement, exhortation, and prayer. He was a true communal participant in the life of the seminary. He refused heat in his room because the students had no heat in theirs. He did his reading in the heated common room with the students and prepared his class notes there. He joined them in outdoor recreations and midnight snacks in the refectory. He was a real shepherd who took on the smell of his sheep.

Seelos's legendary sense of humor found an outlet in the students' "Laughing Society." According to the rules of the society, members might be called upon at any time to tell a joke, after which the members present would determine if it was worthy of laughter. If it was, all the members laughed and continued laughing until signaled to stop. Any violation of the rules would result in prayer penances. Seelos joined the society but soon had to drop out because he couldn't stop laughing on cue, racking up more penances than he could complete in a day.

As prefect, Seelos allowed swimming in the Potomac, walking in the garden during prayer time, and smoking, but only under a doctor's orders. (At the time smoking was believed to be medically therapeutic.) When a student veered from orthodoxy in his words or actions, Seelos attempted to lure him back to the path with kindness and favors. He even permitted a debating society in which points of theology were discussed.

These allowances gained him no friends among his colleagues, who preferred a stringent approach to discipline. They wrote disparagingly of his laxity to the provincial. Seelos never offered a defense. He wrote instead: "I do not want to deceive anybody, but no one believes me when I speak of my perversity and wickedness. According to some I am a saint! In reality I am a thorough scoundrel."[8]

Beyond the seminary staff and faculty, however, he was highly regarded. In the spring of 1860, Father Seelos was being considered for the vacant see of Pittsburgh: the "scoundrel" might be made a bishop! Seelos got wind of the idea and, much like his friend John Neumann, asked his students to start a novena for his deliverance. If successful, he promised them an additional day of recreation.

Unlike Neumann, Seelos's prayers were answered and he was spared the episcopacy. Perhaps it helped that he wrote directly to the pope listing all the reasons why he would make a poor bishop, finishing with, "Because of these things, most Holy Father, I beg most humbly to be freed from such a calamity."[9] True to his promise, Seelos gave the students an extra free day, saying, "I would rather be bishop of my students than Bishop of Pittsburgh."[10]

The war between the North and the South caught Cumberland in the middle. Because of its strategic location, it was almost certain that Confederate forces would attack from Virginia across the river. The seminary was evacuated in 1862. Students and staff moved to Annapolis, thought to be a more defensible city, and Seelos was named superior there.

The following year the federal government began drafting all eligible men to fight for the Union. Seelos agonized over how to keep his students out of the army. His consulters proposed moving the whole student body to Canada, which was rejected. The final plan was simple enough: ordain the lot of them. Baltimore Archbishop Francis Patrick Kenrick performed the deed. They ended up with so many priests that temporary altars had to be built and placed throughout the house for the newly ordained to say Mass.

These measures were stopgap. When the costly campaigns of Fredericksburg and Gettysburg depleted Union forces, new attempts were made to draft the seminarians. Seelos went to Washington and met with Lincoln, but got no satisfaction for his cause. He later met with the Secretary of War, Edwin Stanton, finding him so disagreeable that he later remarked, "Should the Church ever decide to celebrate the feast of a rude rascal, Stanton would qualify easily, even with an octave!"[11] In the end, a friendly draft board back in Cumberland agreed to register all the students and give them deferments.

Despite Father Seelos's good work, the back-channeling and politicking among his detractors continued. He was relentlessly denounced for poor leadership qualities. Finally, in 1862, the provincial wrote that while he personally loved Father Seelos, he felt the man "has not the judgment, wisdom, and reflection, the manner and method to direct the students in the spirit of the Congregation. He does not and cannot understand it."[12] Seelos was dismissed from office, becoming once again a parish priest.

That was fine with him. Seelos was put in charge of a Redemptorist mission band and for the next three years gave parish missions and retreats in Missouri, Illinois, Michigan, Ohio, Pennsylvania, New Jersey, New York, Connecticut, and Rhode Island. He endured the scourges of travel: dirty rail cars, lost luggage, pickpockets, and rude passengers, but he was happy. Preaching missions, the backbone of the Redemptorist charism, was his strong suit. One mission in New York was so successful that extra priests, including the Cardinal Archbishop of New York, John McCloskey, were called in to hear hundreds of confessions. McCloskey admitted later he'd never worked so hard in his life.

In 1865, a new provincial was elected, and Father Seelos was taken out of the mission business and assigned to St. Mary parish in Detroit. Ten months later he was transferred to St. Mary's Assumption Church in New Orleans. With this appointment he had the distinction of having lived in every Redemptorist house in the country. Prophetically, he told a friend this assignment would be his last.

In less than a year, Seelos was dead, brought down by yellow fever— but not before he impressed his own special gifts on the people of New Orleans. Once more his powers of healing manifested. A woman was run over by a streetcar in the city. She survived, badly injured, and remained bedridden for two months. Seelos was called to her side, where he prayed over her and blessed her. The next day she was up and about, crediting the miraculous power in his touch.

In September of 1867, yellow fever visited the city. The fever fell harshly on the Redemptorist rectory. Two priests fell ill, then five. People in the city were dying at an increasing rate of sixty, seventy, then eighty a day. The healthy but weary priests of St. Mary's scrambled to bring the sacraments to the dying.

Seelos visited the sick around the clock while his own health deteriorated. By the end of the month, two Redemptorists had succumbed. The fever finally caught up with Father Seelos, and he reluctantly took to his bed. Two weeks later and near death, he was given the last sacraments. As if the epidemic wasn't enough, a powerful hurricane swept into New Orleans on October 4, the Feast of St. Francis of Assisi. That night, Francis Xavier Seelos died.

After a solemn funeral Mass at St. Mary's the next day, Seelos's body was placed in a crypt near the sanctuary. The church quickly became a site of pilgrimage and remains so to this day. Every year, thousands flock to what is now the shrine of a man the Church calls blessed, to connect with his holiness and seek healing. New Orleans was his last assignment; it promises to be his best.

Today

The National Seelos Shrine and Center with its museum is on Josephine Street in New Orleans, next to St. Mary's Assumption Church. Seelos was laid to rest adjacent to the sanctuary in the church. Volunteers bring Seelos's mission crucifix with its relic to area hospitals. For twenty-five years, an annual healing Mass has been celebrated at the church.

Timeline

1819:	Francis Xavier Seelos born in Füssen, Bavaria, Germany, on January 11
1844:	Seelos ordained a Redemptorist priest; assigned to St. Philomena's in Pittsburgh; Philadelphia rioters burn two Catholic churches and kill thirteen people
1854:	Seelos named rector of St. Alphonsus in Baltimore
1857:	Seelos made prefect of students at the Redemptorist seminary
1861:	Civil War breaks out
1863:	Abraham Lincoln signs Emancipation Proclamation
1865:	Seelos assigned to St. Mary's Assumption in New Orleans
1866:	Second Plenary Council of Baltimore
1867:	Seelos dies of yellow fever on October 4 at age forty-eight

9] Damien (Joseph) de Veuster
(1840–1889)

The Face of Christ at Molokai

Feast: May 10. Venerable: 1977. Beatified: 1995. Canonized: 2009.

Whatever God does is well done.[1]

Leprosy is a word that still has the power to elicit a shudder. It is the epitome of biblical diseases, gathering its deepest connotations from ancient times. Back then, all misfortune was understood as rooted in moral failure. Illness was a sign of sin's ancient curse, brought on by disobedience to God's law. As such, leprosy did more than make people sick. It made them unclean, unfit for the society of their peers.

Beyond devastating the body, leprosy robbed them of their humanity. You suffered other ailments; you *became* a leper. "Leper" was a complete identity, relegating someone to an untouchable race of the doomed. It took a remarkable saint like Francis of Assisi to look into the face of someone afflicted with leprosy and see the suffering Christ. For the sake of Christ, Francis kissed a leper. For Christ's sake, Damien de Veuster became one.

Herein lies the holy perfection of a Belgian peasant described by most contemporaries as an extraordinarily deficient man. Damien's character flaws were many and glaring. His bishops and superiors declared him infuriatingly insubordinate. Members of his Sacred Heart Community of priests found him intolerable to work with. Bishop Hermann Koeckemann of Honolulu, mollified by media worship of Damien after his death, noted snippily that "Saints look better at a distance."[2]

After Damien's first decade at Molokai, his vice-provincial, Father Léonor Fouesnel, couldn't help but slip a criticism into his assessment: "Good man of religion, good priest, excessively devoted to the lepers."[3] Even his best collaborators admitted that Damien undeniably had his failings. Yet to one of them, Ira Dutton, "such faults were consumed like straws in the fire of Damien's charity."[4]

Damien's sanctity is grounded in one immutable fact: He knew the world loathed and shunned those afflicted with leprosy. Simply by going to the colony at Molokai and staying there, Damien's visible presence was a down payment on reform for an otherwise invisible community of suffering. Yet to redeem the humanity of these outcasts and to garner the world's compassionate investment, Damien had to substitute his face for theirs. To do that, he had to be willing to accept the ruin of his attractive features with the knotted, swollen tubercles of *Mycobacterium leprae*. Damien's physical ruin was his spiritual exaltation. It was not a choice his critics were willing to make.

Damien's life began on a farm in Tremelo near Louvain. The De Veusters were Flemish-speaking Belgians and Damien, named Joseph at birth, was the seventh child of eight. Two sisters and a brother found their vocations in the Church before him, thanks in part to their mother Anne-Catherine's deep piety.

Joseph, stocky and strong at thirteen, was being steered to take his father's place on the farm and was removed from school early. By age eighteen, however, in what would prove a characteristic display of stubbornness, Joseph let his parents know their plans for him would have to give way to God's plans. Their youngest son was going to follow his brother Pamphile into religious life.

The brotherly bond is often both affectionate and competitive. Pamphile had entered the Sacred Heart congregation; Joseph aimed to go to the Trappists since he relished hard work. Pamphile disapproved, insisting that his brother join him in Louvain with the Sacred Hearts. Joseph did so without protest.

Ensconced at the seminary, he took the name Brother Damien. It became apparent that Damien, while intelligent enough, was not cut out for the studies required for priesthood. Pamphile was a natural scholar; Damien's truncated education made it hard to keep up. Also, the young man who had imagined himself as a Trappist had little inclination toward contemplation: "With him, things to think about were often turned into things to do," as Damien biographer Gavan Daws observed.[5] The farm boy was vigorously physical; abstract thinking compelled him to sit on his hands.

Four years after Damien joined the Sacred Hearts, Pamphile was recruited for their mission in the Pacific Islands. In 1863 at age twenty-six, Pamphile was well-prepared for missionary work. Damien was only twenty-three at the time and not prepared for ordination. Close to the departure date, however, typhus broke out in Louvain and Pamphile fell ill. Damien leapfrogged his immediate superiors—who knew his inadequacies too well—and wrote to the Congregation's father-general in Paris, asking to be sent to the missions in his brother's place. Permission was granted; Damien would go to Hawaii.

The incompleteness of his preparation would have to be resolved on the far side of the ocean. Arriving in Honolulu after 148 days at sea, Damien was rushed through a two-month diaconate and ordained a priest to make him more useful in the mission territory. Father Damien's later impatience with prolonged baptismal courses, and his willingness to bestow impromptu sacraments on the barely catechized, make sense in the light of his own priesthood, captured on the fly. Damien was always in a hurry to get to the heart of the matter, which was getting a thing done. Protocol maddened him, and pursuing correct channels was beyond his endurance.

When Damien arrived, it had been nearly a century since the explorer James Cook had dubbed this Pacific archipelago the Sandwich Islands after his patron, the fourth Earl of Sandwich. Hawaii had supported a population of a quarter-million natives in the 1770s. Within a century, that number dropped to 50,000 due to the usual contagions that arrived with the Europeans: cholera, smallpox, influenza, measles, and venereal disease.

The first documented case of leprosy on the islands was in 1840. The Hawaiians called it Chinese disease, believing it had come from the west. While the Hawaiian monarchy continued to exert a moral influence on the native community, all practical authority was absorbed by a civil government of white Protestant New Englanders. In the Hawaii that Damien knew, the native population viewed themselves as a community at sunset, waiting for the end of their day with a unified resignation.

The new priest's first assignment was a parish of 350 native Catholics on the island called Hawaii: the biggest of the islands, covered in lava flow from the still-active Kilauea volcano. Father Damien praised this strange landscape "because there is nothing like it in the world to give a correct idea of hell."⁶ To pastor here meant getting used to traveling by land and sea, on horseback, and by foot on an island with no roads. A single tour of preaching and confessions through the parish took six weeks. One village was accessible only by crossing ten ravines followed by a two-thousand-foot climb up a cliff.

Despite the complications of his mission, Damien found time to manage what amounted to a small farm. He had sheep, pigs, and chickens. He kept bees for honey and to make candle wax. He harvested enough beans to share with local religious sisters. He raised his own potatoes, coffee, and tobacco. It was during this assignment that a pipe became his regular "dessert." It would become a necessity in his next parish, on Molokai, to mask the nauseating smell of sickness among his parishioners.

On the island of Hawaii, Father Damien appreciated a blessed lack of supervision. Once a year, Bishop Louis Maigret would visit. The rest of the time, the busy pastor was left to his people, the farm, and the construction of churches. Damien built four churches with his own hands in the decade he was assigned to the Big Island. It was an unusually peaceful time for a self-motivated man who enjoyed manual labor.

Father Damien genuinely liked the Hawaiians, and the feeling was mutual. This priest wasn't like most white people—*haole* in the island language—who disdained the native folk and their customs. This *haole* priest sat on the ground and ate the local dietary staple, *poi*, from a common dish with the *kanaka*, or common folk. Damien also made sense to the *kanaka* because he worked with his hands, and wasn't reluctant to touch the people—an attribute essential to trust and acceptance in Hawaiian culture. Truthfully, their peasant pastor was more like the Hawaiians than the New England Protestants with their sophisticated manners and next-to-godly hygiene. Father Damien's ability to gain the esteem of the "unsanitary" natives was one more reason for civil authorities to mistrust him.

Island politics had long been a complex dance between the royal family and the civil authorities. It was also a duel between the entrenched New England Protestants and the smaller but immutable Catholic missionary presence directed from the bishop's quarters in Honolulu. The islands were a tinderbox waiting for a match to be struck. Into this tense and uneasy environment, leprosy struck with a sudden ubiquity.

From the first diagnosed case, the disease spread rapidly among the native peoples, although it was comparatively rare among the *haole* population. Father Damien, who chose words like tools, clinically recorded a description of the disease that holds enough horror to explain why civil authorities galloped to the notion of segregation: "Leprosy...shows itself first in blackish spots on the skin, especially on the cheeks. In these spots there is no more feeling. After a time, the whole body is covered. Then the sores start, especially on the hands and feet. The toes and fingers are eaten away and give off a fetid odor. Their breath also poisons the air."[7] As distressing as that sounds, leprosy's worst damage occurs after the superficial changes. Once the infiltrating tubercles complete their topical invasion, they burrow into the lungs and interior organs and render the afflicted person weakened to the point of death.

Between five hundred and one thousand native citizens a year were diagnosed with the disease in the late 1800s. Even more were hidden away by families unwilling to surrender their loved ones to *haole* doctors invested with the cruel authority to snatch them away forever.

While what we know as Hansen's disease today is now highly treatable, old-fashioned leprosy was a regular scourge of the tropical world. Since the Middle Ages it had ceased to surface in the European West, so the dominant culture could afford to ignore it. The era of exploration and colonization, however, changed that metric. Free trade across the globe implied the free exchange of diseases. Damien biographer Gavan Daws aptly expresses the bottom line: for the New Englanders of Hawaii, a faraway and forgotten Lazarus had now been abruptly dumped at the rich man's gate, impossible to ignore.

To the non-native community, not greatly impacted by the decision, isolating the afflicted seemed the only reasonable response. To Hawaiians, 5 percent of whom would contract the disease, being separated from spouses, children, and loved ones in the hour of greatest need was an intolerable proposal. To send away a sick daughter into the dubious care of strangers, never to see her again, or to lose a beloved husband to Molokai as surely as to death, was reason enough to evade the law and hide the sick, thereby also exposing the whole community to prolonged risk.

When the first dozen new citizens of Molokai were forced overboard to wade to its un-dockable shores, several were healthy family members who chose to go with their sick as *kokua*, or helpers. The pattern would persist throughout the generations of segregation: Always there were *kokua* who accompanied their loved ones into a virtual death sentence on Molokai.

Molokai was not unpopulated when the sick arrived, and most residents did not flee from their new neighbors. Instead they too chose to become *kokua* with their limited resources. "Great love over fear" was the Hawaiian way, which the ascendant white culture could not seem to appreciate.[8] Rather than withdrawing to save themselves, the Hawaiian instinct was to stay together in what increasingly felt like the twilight of their civilization.

To speak of Molokai requires some nuance; there were actually two distinct communities, one above and one below. On a plateau above steep cliffs lived the white ranchers who owned valuable plantations on the south side of the island. Cut off from the plateau by those cliffs, and from the rest of the world by violent waters, a narrow promontory of four square miles became the geographical prison of the segregated. A mostly barren strip of land, it contained but two sites of interest: the new hospital settlement of Kalawao at the base of the cliffs, and Kalaupapa, a roughly designated landing point for ships.

After nine years of exuberant service on the Big Island, Father Damien appeared ready for a challenge when the bishop announced the call for volunteers for a new mission at Molokai. By 1873, people had been dying in the segregated colony without recourse to the sacraments for seven years—an idea that would have roused Damien's moral outrage. Bishop Maigret had sent visiting priests to minister there on occasion, but as the population of the afflicted grew to a steady five hundred, with continual turnover, the need for full-time attendance was evident. Maigret had no intention of condemning a priest to Molokai, but only sought to organize a relay of regular pastoral care to the colony. Four priests immediately signaled their willingness to go. Damien took the first season.

Within weeks of Damien's departure for Molokai, the Hawaii Evangelical Association signed a statement that would affect the bishop's pastoral plan. Forty-eight Protestant ministers advocated for increased diligence regarding the segregation policy on biblical grounds, "as illustrated by the Mosaic Law in the thirteenth chapter of Leviticus."[9] They vowed to preach frequently on the obligation to isolate the unclean and to condemn anyone who continued to live, eat, or sleep with those afflicted. Because of this, no white Protestant minister would live at Kalawao in Damien's lifetime. This organization's influence on the island Board of Health was significant. Damien was warned that if he remained on Molokai, he must remain segregated himself. It limited the opportunities Damien had to meet with a confessor, something that pained him greatly over the years.

The conviction held by many powerful people on the islands was that leprosy could be contained within a short period: simply corral the sick until they died out. Another popular theory was that leprosy was a contagion spread by immorality—that it was, in fact, the final stage of syphilis contracted through the natives' liberal sexuality. That only a hundred *haole* in a century contracted a disease that killed between five hundred and one thousand Hawaiians a year seemed proof positive of this notion. In either case, the distinct realms of healthy and afflicted were to be inviolably maintained, and it made sense for Damien to volunteer to remain on Molokai as a permanent resident. Bishop Maigret protested only weakly, then let the matter drop.

The Board of Health in Honolulu had made a lot of assumptions when planning the Molokai colony. One was that it would be self-supporting: the residents were expected to engage in subsistence farming. The sick in the settlements at Kalawao could not, would not, and did not conform to that model. The Board of Health seemed incredulous at the realization that it would have to provide food for the sick into the foreseeable future. Also, adequate housing had not been provided. The rapidly increasing numbers of afflicted were not motivated to build homes for themselves. The hospital was no more than a rough shelter, and for half of the colony's existence, a resident doctor was not provided. Clothing was budgeted at six dollars a year per person. The drug budget was one cent a month per patient.

All of this Father Damien found out only upon his arrival in his new parish. He also inherited the badly weathered church of St. Philomena erected by an earlier Sacred Heart priest. Damien slept under a pandanus tree near the church and ate off the surface of a rock until he was able to construct a small house nearby. And then, characteristically, Damien got to work and didn't stop for the next sixteen years. He made it his business to visit each sick parishioner every week—which is to say, *every* parishioner—Catholic or not. It took him nearly five days a week, dawn until dark, to make these rounds. He offered Mass three times on Sundays at Kalawao, and sometimes crossed over to Kalaupapa for a Mass or prayer service. Though only one-third of Kalawao's six hundred residents were Catholics at the opening census, within three months Damien counted nearly four hundred catechumens.

One early priority became the cemetery, and the formation of a funeral society. Since everyone in his parish was to leave the community by way of the cemetery, Damien erected a cross and built a white picket fence around the sanctified ground. As Daws notes, this little touch reflected the pastor's sensibility that the graveyard "should be as little a horror as possible, at the end of a life of horrors."[10] Damien built makeshift instruments and trained musicians, raising up a choir that learned to sing Mozart. He also built innumerable coffins. Processions to the cemetery took place three times a week, with as much dignity as possible. Damien buried his entire parish in the first five years. He would bury his community three times over during his time as their pastor.

The need for a home for orphaned children at Kalawao was obvious. Some place for the elderly and for unprotected women who could be preyed upon was also necessary. As Damien formed plans, he also begged his bishop and his Sacred Heart superiors for a companion to come share the work. He asked for religious sisters to educate the girls and supervise the women. Damien asked for money, boards and nails, and mostly for a priest collaborator.

Three Sacred Heart priests were sent to him over the sixteen years: one mentally volatile, one openly hostile to Damien, and a third too sick to be of much use. Damien finally passed over his superiors and started making appeals for money and help to the outside world through the press, tapping into an unexpected wellspring. Money flowed into the mission, and so did his most useful companions: Father Louis-Lambert Conrardy from the Oregon Indian missions; layman Ira Barnes Dutton, veteran of the Civil War; and layman James Sinnett of Ireland.

As Father Damien became the world's most beloved beggar, his superiors now found fault with his ungovernable celebrity. Bishop Koeckemann, who succeeded Maigret upon his death in 1882, and vice-provincial Fouesnel both scolded Damien privately and publicly as lacking humility, patience, poverty, and obedience. In a final remarkable snub, when the day finally came for the world to mourn the loss of a man largely viewed as a moral giant, neither of his immediate superiors would attend Damien's funeral.

Damien had few illusions about his own chances of contracting leprosy. From his earliest days in the colony he noticed an itching in his skin. Sores would come and go. In the 1880s he developed a pain in his left leg, and two years later lost feeling in his left foot. After unconsciously scalding his foot in 1885, he submitted to a full examination that confirmed his affliction. By the end of the year, the appearance of his face told the world he now shared the fate of his parishioners. News of the diagnosis went worldwide in 1886. Anne-Catherine de Veuster heard a report of her son's condition from a Belgian newspaper. The shock of the report, grossly exaggerated, ended her life. She died clasping a picture of the Blessed Mother and one of her son.

The man once described as "vigorous, forceful…a jack of all trades, carpenter, mason, baker, farmer, Medico, and nurse"[11] continued his rounds with a still-passionate intensity despite diminished energy. In October of 1888, a weakened Father Damien fell at the altar and could not finish the Mass. As if in answer to a long-lost and finally rerouted prayer, the Franciscan Sisters he had been begging for arrived the next month to take up the mission.

After sixteen years of mostly solitary efforts, Damien gained a harvest of allies for Molokai in his last few months: the Franciscan Sisters, Father Conrardy, and the two laymen Dutton and Sinnett. Damien considered them all his *Nunc Dimittus,* the Prayer of Simeon he recited from his breviary each night: "Lord, now you let your servant go in peace. Your word has been fulfilled."

Just before Easter in 1889, Damien took to his bed. On April 14 he was aware of two figures with him constantly, though no one else could see them. After his death on April 15, the Sisters dressed him in his vestments and prepared a coffin for the one who had presided over thousands of funerals. The band that played at all Kalawao funerals led the procession to the cemetery. Father Damien slept once more under his pandanus tree. His community was in good hands.

Today

Hansen's disease has been inexpensively controllable since the 1940s. Drugs introduced in the 1980s made treatment without segregation possible. From a peak of five million new cases annually in the nineteenth century, newly diagnosed patients are now fewer than 250,000 a year worldwide. The populations of India, Brazil, and Indonesia are especially afflicted. In 1936, the Belgian government controversially removed Father Damien's body from Molokai to Leuven, Belgium. After his beatification in 1995, Damien's hand was returned and re-interred at his original gravesite at Kalaupapa.

Timeline

1840:   Joseph de Veuster born in Belgium on January 3
1859:   De Veuster joins Sacred Hearts under the name Damien

1860:   U.S. Civil War begins
1864:   Damien comes to the Big Island of Hawaii
1866:   First twelve people with leprosy isolated at Molokai
1873:   Damien arrives at Molokai; scientist Hansen identifies bacillus causing leprosy
1884:   Damien diagnosed with leprosy
1888:   Father Conrardy and James Sinnett volunteer; Franciscan Sisters arrive
1889:   Father Damien dies on April 15 at Kalawao, at age forty-nine
1898:   Hawaii annexed to the United States
1941:   Cure for Hansen's disease discovered
1969:   Forced leprosy segregation policy ends in Hawaii

10] Marianne (Barbara Koob) Cope
(1838–1918)

Angel of Mercy to the Sick

Feast: January 23. Venerable: 2004. Beatified: 2005. Canonized: 2012.

Do not allow it to trouble you and when the thought comes to you drive it from your mind and remember: you will never be a leper, nor will any Sister of our order.[1]

Some of us have a tough time doing the right thing—especially when the taks is difficult. Fewer of us manage to do so without complaining. Almost none of us do it cheerfully. These are the great virtues of Marianne Cope, the other hero of Hawaii, who spent half a lifetime caring for leprosy sufferers. She didn't do it alone, but with a team of Franciscan sisters, many deserving of their own saintly titles. That Cope was nearly unknown during the years Father Damien was honored throughout the world reflected her plan precisely. She insisted it was never about her; it was about the work.

Barbara Koob was born in Heppenheim, Germany. When she was two, her parents emigrated with four children to America and settled in Utica, New York. During that century of immigration, benevolent associations in Utica took good care of German-speaking newcomers. Peter Koob became a naturalized citizen fifteen years later, and his children automatically received citizenship with him. Gradually most of the family adopted the phonetically similar name Cope.

Many boys and most girls of Barbara's generation didn't attend school after the eighth grade. As five more children were born to the family in Utica, Barbara was needed at home anyway. She learned to be efficient and industrious there, adopting the Cope family trait of doing things cheerfully. This would be especially valued in a household that endured many losses. Back in Germany, Peter Koob's first wife had nine children, losing seven before her death. Two of Barbara's full brothers also died before she was out of her teens.

Barbara developed the gift, often seen in children from big families, of being unusually empathetic in dealing with people. Managing a household with impeccable organizational skills would also serve her well when she became the principal of schools, the administrator of hospitals, and the head of her religious order.

Barbara enjoyed a natural loveliness: dark eyes, fine features, and a perennially pleasant expression. Later, even as a fully habited religious sister, her serene beauty would enchant the royalty of Hawaii, government officials, unsympathetic Calvinists, rebellious patients, and a few problematic sisters.

By the age of fifteen, Barbara desired to enter the convent. But because her family needed her, she remained at home another nine years, working in a factory and bringing home her paycheck. Then the Franciscan Sisters from Philadelphia opened a convent in Utica. Their superior, Mother Bernardina Dorn, deeply attracted Barbara. Within two years Mrs. Cope gave her blessing on her daughter's decision to join up and become Sister Mary Anna, eventually shortened to Marianne.

In the same year as Marianne's profession, a young man named Damien de Veuster was ordained on an island across the world. It would be another twenty-two years until they met. By then, their lives would already be linked by a dedication to a population most people considered only with horror.

Sister Marianne climbed an ascending ladder of achievement. In 1865 she began, as most religious sisters did, teaching elementary schoolchildren, in Syracuse, in Rome to the northeast, and in Oswego on the shore of Lake Ontario. Her good judgment, fidelity to the task, and ability to provide benign direction led to her promotion to principal of two schools. Early on she also headed the convents where she lived. When Mother Bernardina took sick, the priest provincial who guided their Franciscan chapter did not hesitate to appoint Sister Marianne as the community's acting superior.

Mother Bernardina had visited the sick of Utica from the time her community arrived in town. Soon she opened a small hospital next to the parish church. In this she stayed true to the work she had done in Philadelphia under the encouragement of Bishop John Neumann. The need for accessible medical care was great. Typhus, malaria, and tuberculosis were common. At the Franciscan hospital in Utica, no distinction was made on the basis of belief, nationality, or color. This was a bold charter in 1866.

The term *hospital* might be misleading. In the mid-nineteenth century, a hospital was a place that offered "a bed to lie in and to die in."[2] Few treatments that doctors administered were curative. Healing depended on the body's own defenses, as the link between microorganisms and disease was only starting to be explored. Specialists were recommending sanitation in health care, but many doctors still did not wash with soap and water between patient visits. Sister Marianne, however, heartily adopted the new hygienic practices when hospital work came under her supervision. She also became a respected apothecary; later, in Hawaii, she would be considered a professional druggist in the terms of the times.

Not long after Sister Marianne returned to Utica to cover for Mother Bernardina, she was abruptly transferred again by the priest provincial. This time it was to Syracuse to take over administration of St. Joseph's Hospital. This presented a problem: another sister of the community already headed up that institution. Sister Dominica was a personality variously described as stormy, masculine, and pugilistic—the precise opposite of her replacement. These two sisters were told to trade assignments; this mandate gained Sister Marianne a devoted enemy.

When Mother Bernardina recovered from her illness, she still required assistance in governing the community, so Sister Marianne occupied three full-time positions for the next three years: secretary-general of the province, mistress of novices, and hospital administrator. Her devotion to Mother Bernardina made this overextension bearable; what made it a "cheerful" burden was Marianne's own quiet determination.

Apart from the duties within her community, she supervised all hospital personnel: doctors, nurses, and volunteers, as well as patients and visitors. She was responsible for buildings and furnishings, financial reports and fundraising. She wrote endless thank-you notes for barrels of flour and pounds of crackers. And she did her best to vanish behind each task.

Her service within the Franciscan community contributed to the refinement of her skills. Working side by side with Mother Bernardina,

Sister Marianne gained a keen appreciation of women's psychology and how to honor each sister's dignity when making decisions about her future. Just as Marianne treated patients at the hospital as individuals, she recognized each sister as a woman with a unique set of gifts and needs. Mother Bernardina also taught her assistant how to deal with men, which required patience and tact while navigating their authority, egos, and ambitions. This helped greatly in negotiations with priests, bishops, doctors, and legislators in years to come.

Cope biographer and Franciscan Sister Mary Laurence Hanley neatly describes the situation: "In the perennial contesting between religious women wanting to manage their own business and wilful [*sic*] men determined to mind it for them, she learned how to appease superiors in the masculine hierarchy without ever yielding too much control to them."[3] Every female saint working within the structures of the church embraced this lesson one way or another in order to succeed in her divinely appointed commission.

An example of this diplomacy is seen in the case of a Sister Bonaventure, lured from the community by a priest hoping to install her as superior of a house he was starting in New Jersey. He applied for the dispensation of her vows, which Mother Bernardina accepted. Four months later, Bonaventure regretted the scheme and asked to return to the Franciscans in Utica. Permission was granted. And a good thing too, as Bonaventure would be an indispensable member of the convoy to Hawaii in a few years' time.

The same graciousness was shown in the thornier matter of Sister Dominica, late of St. Joseph's Hospital in Syracuse. When her "nemesis" Sister Marianne eventually became superior of the order in 1877, Sister Dominica was restored to her position at the hospital. Mother Marianne, at the age of thirty six, now orchestrated the ministries of sixty-two sisters, nine schools, and two hospitals. Her authority over Dominica continued to plague the more brittle woman.

After four years of obstruction and insolence, Sister Dominica cracked, deserting her responsibilities and the community, returning to her family. Predictably, a year later Dominica was back, asking for readmittance. Not only was she reinstated; by showing great sensitivity to Dominica's dignity throughout the process, Mother Marianne won over her old enemy. Sister Dominica gave more years of faithful service to her community and her superior.

Then, out of the blue, in 1883 a letter arrived that would change many lives. Father Léonor Fouesnel wrote Mother Marianne from the Kingdom of Hawaii. He begged for her assistance, stating that the need was so great and pitiable, mentioning a hospital built and waiting for her sisters. He wrote of shed tears and sore distress, promising carriages, daily Mass, no government interference, and permission to have the Blessed Sacrament in their convent. Travel to the Sandwich Islands would be reimbursed; salaries would be paid. There were "other conditions" too delicate to put in writing. Would she consider this desperate appeal?

The letter was long and emotional, but raised more questions than it answered. Mother Marianne didn't know where the Sandwich Islands were, nor how this hospital would be supported. She had no idea how many of this priest's promises would prove to be blurred truths or outright lies. The one crucial "condition" missing from the letter was that this "delicate" appeal was on behalf of victims of leprosy. What Fouesnel didn't say was more important than all the rest.

Mother Marianne couldn't know that Fouesnel was an archenemy of another dedicated religious under his purview: Father Damien. She couldn't guess that fifty other Catholic institutions had received the same "personal" appeal that she did. All she knew was that the letter awakened her compassion. She invited Fouesnel to come to New York with his proposal. She was the only one of the fifty recipients who did.

In late nineteenth-century Hawaii, Catholics were the second largest religious group, far poorer and less powerful than the Protestants, who ran the government and marginalized the weak royal family. Bishop Hermann Koeckemann in Honolulu did want the hospital, called Kakaako, to be staffed by Catholic sisters but had no means to foot the expense. Neither he nor his envoy, Fouesnel, trusted the civil government's proposal to back the institution. At the heart of their mistrust was the man promoting the enterprise: Walter Murray Gibson, known on the islands as "the minister of everything."[4]

Gibson is a character belonging more properly to fiction than to history. Through many careers he roamed from Canada to Central America. He was at sea for a time, and also a trader, gold hunter, and smuggler. He championed the Mormon cause during their season of persecution in the United States by establishing a colony for them in Central Oceana. It didn't work out; the Mormons excommunicated him. He quickly restyled himself as savior of the native Hawaiians, making himself indispensable to the royal family and secular government. In 1873, Gibson raised a public cry for a "royal soul" to shine forever in service to Hawaii's leper colony. That appeal had originally pushed Bishop Louis Maigret, Koeckemann's predecessor, to organize the mission to Molokai, resulting in Father Damien's presence there.

By all accounts, Gibson was never in it for the money. What he craved was attention, playing the royals against the civil authorities, Catholics against Protestants, taking no clear side but his own. When Bishop Koeckemann commissioned Fouesnel to procure sisters for the medical mission, Walter Murray Gibson was in the background, hinting that Anglican sisters might beat Catholics to the islands, thereby giving the Protestants the upper hand. This Koeckemann could not abide.

While powerful men played political chess in Hawaii, Father Fouesnel was weeping in Mother Marianne's parlor in Syracuse, finally bringing himself to utter the word that had been lacking in his letter: *leprosy*. Overwhelmed by the living tragedy painted for her, Mother Marianne accepted the mission. Nearly every one of her novices asked to go, as did many of the sisters.

The Franciscans' priest-provincial, Father Joseph Lesen, was appalled at the news. He insisted that details had been withheld, that more needed to be discussed, proper channels consulted, written promises procured. Fouesnel had originally asked for six sisters, and already he was angling for seven or eight. Lesen wanted letters from Bishop Koeckemann himself, outlining the responsibility of the local church to these women. Mother Marianne only repeated that thirty-five sisters had already cheerfully agreed to go to the Sandwich Islands. Even Sister Dominica had volunteered. In the end, six sisters, including Bonaventure, accompanied Mother Marianne to Hawaii.

The sisters were royally received in Honolulu, quite literally: the King and Queen sent representatives and a royal carriage. A parade followed them to the cathedral, where the bishop waited to give his blessing. The church was full, music played, and the Franciscan Sisters were overcome by this warm Hawaiian welcome. The Protestants, too, were suitably impressed.

Walter Murray Gibson himself stood in the gathering, losing his heart to these Angels of Mercy at first sight: "so austere, so pure, so ethereal, so beautiful."[5] He would one day give a ring to his precious Mother Marianne, engraved with their initials joined by a heart, citing Ruth 1:16–17. By then she would be diplomatic enough to receive it— and never wear it. Gibson would become her most volatile ally, as she grew skilled at Hawaiian politics.

Of course, after all the introductory fuss, it was clear no convent awaited them, and none of the initial promises had been kept. Sacred Heart sisters took in the Franciscans while their convent was built, adjoining the Honolulu hospital compound that would be their mission. A low parapet was intended to separate the world of the Franciscans from the patients they served; in time even this slight division would be removed. Their inclusion in the isolated world of leprosy sufferers would be nearly absolute.

Native Hawaiians speak of *mana*, the divine power that all created things contain and all people possess to some degree. They agreed Mother Marianne had very powerful *mana*. When the Hawaiian Queen came calling, she was moved to tears that this houseful of women would leave their country forever to come and care for her sick people. The Queen became an ally Mother Marianne could count on in this foreign land.

The Hawaiian Board of Health had established the hospital, Kakaako, as a sorting station for persons suspected of leprosy. Several other illnesses mimicked the early symptoms, ranging from rashes to tumors. If leprosy was eventually confirmed, the patient was to be shipped on to Molokai. Others were to be treated at Kakaako and released. The system rarely functioned as planned. For one thing, families used their influence to keep their loved ones at Kakaako, where they still had access to them, no matter what the diagnosis. For another, patients sequestered with leprosy sufferers were prone to develop the disease. Kakaako had been designed for one hundred patients; it soon held twice as many.

Kakaako was run like a prison. Its warden was Dr. George L. Fitch, a moralist who viewed sickness rather biblically; that is, he believed people who got sick probably earned it. He rejected the recent Norway findings about the bacterial root of leprosy. Fitch was convinced leprosy was actually the end-stage of syphilis, contracted by sexual promiscuity. He asserted that was why licentious Hawaiians and Catholic priests like Damien caught the disease.

Dr. Fitch repeated his theory so often and so publicly that it was regarded by many as fact. When a minister in California publically questioned Damien's moral behavior in a particularly salacious way, renowned author (and weary tuberculosis sufferer) Robert Louis Stevenson would feel morally obliged to publish an open letter denouncing such character assassination to the world.

If Kakaako was a prison, its principal guard was the sadist Henry Van Giesen. He had arrived there originally as a *kokua*, or healthy helper, for his afflicted wife. As she lost her beauty to the disease, he grew to hate her and all the affected population, tormenting and torturing them without reprisal. The Franciscan sisters inherited both Dr. Fitch and the steward Van Giesen with no authority to remove them. Even worse, the men of Kakaako routinely preyed on the women and children. Each night as the sisters retreated to their convent, the hospital behind them turned into a brothel of the willing and unwilling alike.

Within days, the sisters saw it all: the victimized, traumatized, listless patients of a disease that held enough horror of its own. They saw the filth and the flies, inhaled the terrible odor of rotting flesh, experienced the atmosphere of shame and blame, and witnessed the barren landscape that those condemned behind the walls of Kakaako would endure until death. What the sisters saw, most of all, was that much good could be done there.

One sister was assigned full-time responsibilities within the convent, to ensure a sanitary food supply and environment for the community. Another sister was set in charge of dressing patients' sores, which she did for ten hours daily. The rest of the sisters, including Mother Marianne, got to work scrubbing Kakaako from one end of the enclosure to the other. They did it all without modern equipment like gloves and masks. They washed frequently, and trusted Mother Marianne's promise to them that no Franciscan sister would ever contract leprosy from this ministry. They never did.

As the environment was transformed around the patients of Kakaako and their suffering daily tended, they began to rally from the land of death. Their lives grew longer, better, and sweeter-smelling. Unlike doctors who left salves on posts and refused to approach the afflicted, these sisters were willing to wash maggots off wounds, cut away rotted flesh, and apply ointments personally. No one had loved a leprosy sufferer with such humanity except for Father Damien, who had gone to Molokai ten years earlier. But this wasn't Molokai. No one had loved the sick of Kakaako at all.

As the sisters worked to the brink of exhaustion within the hospital, Mother Marianne also worked the external systems that had invented this hell. Neither the bishop nor Gibson would define the authority the sisters exercised over the institution to which they were committed. The Board of Health had no answers. None of the men in charge could see their way to handing control of a government-funded hospital to a group of Catholic nuns. Instead, it was proposed that the sisters staff an additional hospital in Maui for non-leprosy sufferers as well. Considering the exertions they already endured, it was an outrageous proposition. Trying to perceive the angle behind this gambit, Mother Marianne accepted. Within the first year, she took two sisters with her to Maui.

With their superior absent, the other Franciscans did their best to keep the volatile situation at Kakaako under control. But the malicious Van Giesen grew bolder, causing greater harm than before, even threatening the security of the sisters. The bishop recalled Mother Marianne to Honolulu before the year was out to pacify the population. She laid down the law for the bishop, Gibson, and the Board of Health in tones low and sweet but clear. If Van Giesen wasn't removed immediately, if the sisters weren't given administrative authority over Kakaako, they would leave Hawaii.

Van Giesen was removed. The sisters were given administrative control of their mission. A wall was built to separate the women and children of Kakaako from the men. Sometime that eventful year, Father Damien came to Honolulu to attend the blessing of their convent chapel. He had already lived at the settlement on Molokai for over a decade and faced the same vulnerability of the women and children there. He had hammered his superiors with his ceaseless requests for sisters to help on Molokai.

After seeing the results of the sisters' work at Kakaako, Damien began to send his "clean" girls back to Honolulu to reside at the new Kapiolani Home for Girls, opened by the sisters and financed by the Queen. Such an institution was necessary, since children born at the settlement were at risk of developing their parents' disease.

A year later, Father Damien himself was in need of medical attention. The leprosy he had suspected for four years had been confirmed, and a nerve in his leg and foot was already destroyed. He came to Kakaako for a week of experimental treatments, and again had the chance to talk—and talk and talk—about Molokai. He drove Mother Marianne and his attending sisters to the limits of their charity. But after a dozen years as the lone moral leader at Molokai, doing everything the sisters at Kakaako were doing—visiting the sick, dressing sores—as well as building houses and coffins, administering sacraments, hearing confessions, and burying the dead, Damien had rather a lot to say.

Walter Murray Gibson found this priest's presence in the sisters' compound unbearable. Gibson was terrorized by the idea that his beautiful sisters, Mother Marianne especially, would follow Damien to his foul island. But Damien returned to Molokai alone. Gibson had his ethereal Franciscans all to himself again. Yet nothing lasts forever. With the collapse of the Hawaiian kingdom in 1887, Gibson would be banished from the islands. Fleeing to San Francisco, he would retire to a hospital there run by the Sisters of Mercy. Gibson died of tuberculosis surrounded by the purity he worshipped so dearly.

It was a new day in Hawaii: The decision was made to rid Honolulu of the taint of disease by closing Kakaako and sending all remaining patients to Molokai. The Franciscan sisters were given permission to go with them.

While new Franciscan recruits from Syracuse had routinely arrived in Hawaii during the mission years, many had served exclusively at the Maui hospital in routine health care, or at the Kapiolani Home with girls who were free of disease. The thought of Molokai frightened these sisters. Even those who had served at Kakaako found fresh horror at the idea of the deepening isolation. Some applied to return to Syracuse. Bonaventure was needed to run Maui; others elected to remain in Honolulu. Mother Marianne took only two sisters with her to Molokai: Vincent and Leopoldina, both later recruits. Sister Vincent endured Molokai for twelve difficult years before leaving the island and her community of sisters. Sister Leopoldina would become the great chronicler of the Mother she revered, spending four decades of her life on Molokai.

By 1888, Mother Marianne's health was wearing thin. Although it was never discussed, she had suffered from lifelong pulmonary tuberculosis, possibly contracted early in her time at Utica. By the time she boarded the boat to Molokai, the illness was sapping her strength. Sister Leopoldina tells of bleak first impressions of the barren Kalaupapa promontory, their new home. She also writes poignantly of the ruin of Father Damien's body, too sick now to serve as confessor for their community; they had to bring a healthy priest with them.

As usual, there was plenty of work to engage the sisters upon arrival. They ran the Charles R. Bishop Home for Unprotected Leper Girls and Women at Kalaupapa, teaching domestic arts: sewing, cooking, cleaning, and laundry. Mother Marianne made hats and dresses for the girls, exhibiting a flair for colors and bows. The sisters bought books and Christmas presents for the children with the twenty dollar monthly stipend they had each received since arriving in Hawaii.

The sisters also guarded the females from routine raids from the men's side of the peninsula, which was governed by the ailing Damien and his assistants. Courtship supervised by the sisters was permitted between the two settlements, and a few marriages did take place on Molokai. When things were quiet, Mother Marianne planted vegetables, useful trees, and flowering shrubs. Father Damien had never had time for landscaping, but under Mother Marianne's care, Kalaupapa found its beauty.

Father Damien rarely visited Kalaupapa anymore, remaining at the Kalawao settlement miles away. He refused to enter the sisters' parlor when invited: it was forbidden, he demurred, as he was a leper. Yet once Sister Leopoldina spied the poor priest in the garden, on his knees near the sisters' chapel at the wall nearest the Blessed Sacrament. He would not pollute their sanctuary, but offered his prayers outside. Tears sprang to her eyes.

When Damien looked up, he saw the traces of her tears, and asked with innocent tenderness, "Did someone hurt your feelings?"[6] His remarkable compassion burned into Leopoldina's memory. The next time she saw Father Damien would be at his funeral.

Only months after the sisters' arrival, news of Father Damien's death reached their side of the promontory. The sisters dressed his coffin with black serge, satin pleating, lace, and silver tacks. They made armbands for the funeral party. After Damien joined "his children" in the cemetery, Mother Marianne faced new challenges.

The Home for Boys at Kalawao needed a firmer hand to run it than Damien's heirs were showing, and the sisters tried to administer both homes before admitting defeat. Several Sacred Heart brothers from Damien's Belgian community, including his elder brother, Pamphile de Veuster, were installed to undertake the task. But Pamphile, now in his fifties, was too accustomed to academic life to face the intellectual tedium of Molokai. He returned to Belgium.

Hawaii was annexed to the United States before Mother Marianne's death. While she never returned to the U.S., the country returned to her. Her final years were increasingly disabled, and faithful Leopoldina remained at her side, pushing her wheelchair. In 1918, Mother Marianne died as graciously and unobtrusively as she had lived. She was buried on Molokai near an orange grove she planted. Five of her sisters remained in service on the islands, most of them giving forty years or more to their mission.

Today

Sixty-three Sisters of St. Francis followed Mother Marianne to Kalaupapa on Molokai to care for people with Hansen's disease and their families. To date, not one sister has contracted the disease. Now known as the Sisters of St. Francis of the Neumann Communities, headquartered in Syracuse, New York, they continue to work in health care, education, social services, and spiritual centers in twelve states, Washington, D.C., Puerto Rico, Africa, and Peru. The Shrine and Museum of Saint Marianne Cope is located at the St. Anthony Convent in Syracuse where the saint's body now rests.

Timeline

1838:	Barbara Koob born in Heppenheim, Germany on January 23
1840:	Koob family settles near Utica, New York
1860:	Civil War begins
1862:	Barbara Cope enters Franciscans as Mary Anna
1869:	Cope named administrator of St. Joseph Hospital, Syracuse
1872:	Oliver Wendell Holmes advises doctors to wash hands
1873:	Father Damien arrives at Molokai; Hansen identifies leprosy bacillus
1877:	Cope named superior of her community
1883:	Cope approached to run Kakaako hospital in Honolulu
1884:	Maui hospital staffed by sisters

1887: Walter Murray Gibson driven from Hawaii
1888: Franciscan Sisters arrive on Molokai
1889: Father Damien dies
1898: Hawaii annexed to the United States
1918: Mother Marianne dies of tuberculosis at Molokai on August 9, at age eighty

11] Frances Xavier (Maria Francesca) Cabrini (1850–1917)

Teacher of the Heart

Feast: November 13. Venerable: 1937. Beatified: 1938. Canonized: 1946.

The Heart of Jesus does things in such a hurry that I can barely keep up with Him![1]

Maria Francesca Cabrini almost drowned as a child and suffered a lifelong fear of water. This didn't prevent her from crossing the ocean dozens of times in pursuit of souls, one of the most well-traveled women of her generation. Captains christened her a sea wolf for her courage demonstrated on stormy voyages. Pope Pius X dubbed her "the Apostle of the Gospel," and after her death, Pius XII proclaimed her "Patroness of Immigrants." The Italian Ambassador to the United States, Baron Mayor des Planches, insisted, "Mother Cabrini was a great man!"[2] He meant it as a compliment.

This little Italian woman, living in a fragile body, had a stout heart ablaze with divine love. Though she was frequently opposed by churchmen and business leaders, her adversaries all soon learned the same lesson: that resistance was futile. "There is no joking with Mother Cabrini," politicians admitted ruefully in New Orleans,[3] echoing sentiments of the powerful in every city she claimed with her Missionary Sisters of the Sacred Heart.

Telling Cabrini's story itself seems futile: she tells it better than any biographer in letters composed during ocean voyages throughout twenty-eight years as a missionary. Her prose is painterly and informed, wise and funny, the pages sprinkled with a close knowledge of Scripture that few priests of her day enjoyed.

Cabrini had a geographer's curiosity about the world, which was exercised each time she sailed away from Italy. She also had a mystic's vision that seeped into time, compelling her to make each hour count for something grand in eternity. She routinely interpreted exterior wonders through the interior world of the spirit. In terms of productive action, there is hardly another saint in the canon to match Mother Cabrini.

It all seemed so improbable at the start. Born in Lombardy before there was a proper nation of Italy, Maria Francesca was the tenth of eleven children. This baby arrived so frail she was expected to die, but when she survived, her older sister Rosa committed herself to training her in the faith. Little Maria Francesca transformed her dolls into convents of nuns which had to conform to her strict rule of life. She picked violets to sail in paper boats as missionary flowers bound for China. Falling into the water with her "missionaries" one day, Cabrini developed bronchitis that nearly killed her. Sometime in those early years she also contracted malaria that wracked her with lifelong fevers and periods of near-total infirmity. Both of her parents died before she was twenty. Yet somehow their delicate daughter persisted.

At thirteen Cabrini applied to a school run by the Daughters of the Sacred Heart to become a certified teacher. Her long-term goal was to enter religious life, but after granting her diploma, the sisters declined to accept this bright and fervent new teacher whose spirit was so willing, but whose body was so evidently weak. Other communities also viewed Cabrini as a poor investment. In the end, the joke was on them, as Cabrini was destined to personally found a mind-boggling sixty-seven institutions, one for every year she lived. For the moment, she resigned herself to teach and wait on God for the rest.

Two years later, a smallpox epidemic struck the region. Cabrini the teacher became a health care worker. Contracting smallpox from her patients, she did not endure a single disfiguring scar from the disease. She resumed teaching, being moved about from Sant'Angelo to Vidardo to Codogno along with pastors who admired her efficiency and preferred to keep her successes in their own parishes. For eight years she went where directed and fulfilled clerical expectations, always keeping an eye on Asia and the missionary life to which she felt drawn with every fiber of her being. Finally she met a Monsignor who told her frankly: "I do not know of an institute for missionary sisters; found one."[4] Cabrini didn't need to hear it twice.

The Missionary Sisters of the Sacred Heart—or the Institute, as she always preferred to call it—was an aberration from the start. Prelates balked at the term *missionary* being applied to a group of schoolteachers who had never left Italy. It was an accident of history: within the decade Mother Cabrini and six of her sisters would be on their way to America. Cabrini embraced the name Xavier to confirm her resolve to follow the great missionary saint Francis Xavier to Asia. Her sisters would go there one day; her personal mission would be surprisingly different.

In the early days at Codogno, the new missionaries ate their meals on benches, sharing one fork and one spoon around the table. In each new venture, their accommodations would be similarly poor and often worse. Yet the community radiated the spirit of their foundress, who had "loosened the chains of psychological conditioning" and allied herself with God, as Sacred Heart biographer Mother Saverio de Maria explains.[5] Like their Mother, the sisters would help with the cooking, the wardrobe, the henhouse, or the administration of the community as needed. They would endure seasickness and bug-infested beds, eat suspicious-looking new foods, and do it all with an absolute dedication to their Institute's queen of virtues: obedience.

Mirroring Cabrini's personality, the sisters practiced continual adoration of the Sacred Heart of Jesus by means of the gospel of work. With divine love as the model, there could be no humiliating corrections of sisters or students, no sarcasm or rude words, and no corporal punishments of any kind. Criticism of others was forbidden. Interior self-denial was emphasized, and exterior physical mortifications discouraged. Having been turned away from religious communities because of her weakness, Cabrini set other criteria for admission: she sought frank, dynamic people with bright, smiling faces as her postulants.

As a result of its unique spirit, women flocked to join this Institute full of joyful sisters. The convent at Codogno was expanded several times before the priest overseer objected, recommending a cap on admissions to the order. With the community praying daily for new recruits, this sounded crazy to Cabrini, with her missionary ambitions. She told the priest it was "harmful to the work of God" to restrict the novitiate.[6] If the house was too small, all the more reason to begin sending sisters abroad.

Money was always an issue for a community with no network of financial support. Yet the means seemed to fall from heaven when needed. When a creditor arrived at the door and there was nothing in the drawer with which to pay him, Cabrini directed the sister to look in the drawer a second time, and a package of new bills was discovered. When the wine merchant showed up and the drawer remained empty, Cabrini told the sister to check her pocket. The exact price to cover the bill was found there. These stories illustrate a grounding Cabrini principle: mistrust the self, put unlimited trust in God.

This principle was put to the test in 1887 when Mother Cabrini decided it was time to found a school for her missionaries at the heart of the Church in Rome. Without credentials or letters of introduction, she traveled to the Eternal City to discover that boundless faith was not a strategy much in keeping with local practices.

A cardinal informed Cabrini she needed 500,000 lire to promote her cause. When she insisted that Our Lady of Grace was the real foundress of her Institute, the cardinal replied that if Our Lady of Grace came up with 500,000 lire, he would take that as a sign of God's favor. Cabrini took refuge with another religious foundress in the city, Mother Mary of the Passion, who befriended her as a kindred spirit. While clergy back home provided the proper letters and recommendations, Cabrini put her trust in Mother Mary's words regarding the cardinal: "Calm yourself; God will change his heart."[7] The next time Cabrini saw him, the prelate received her warmly—and gave her permission to found not one, but two, houses in Rome.

While in Rome, Mother Cabrini was approached by the Bishop of Piacenza who was anxious to send religious to assist the rapidly growing Italian immigrant population in New York. With her heart set on China, Cabrini was skeptical, especially since the proposal involved accepting the direction and support of American clergy—a fate that jeopardized the independence of the Institute. Besides, Cabrini viewed the United States as "a place where everything abounds that attracts the eye, tempts the heart, and weakens the meditative spirit."[8] She felt her sisters would be more spiritually effective in lands more empty of appeal, such as China or Africa.

Yet Cabrini was bound by her allegiance to that infallible virtue, obedience. She preferred not to make decisions born of self-will, but to abandon herself to the divine will as expressed through the authority of the Church. If the Archbishop of New York really needed Italian sisters to run an orphanage and a school, perhaps this was God's will laid before her.

Time, too, had become a factor: her fevers had returned, and the doctor was predicting she had two years to live. Her friend Mother Mary of the Passion affirmed the New York mission. Still, Cabrini was determined to let the pope decide. When she met with Pope Leo XIII that first time, she didn't mention America. She simply impressed on him that, in seven years, her Institute had grown to 145 women who were ready for the missions.

Pope Leo knew the situation in America quite well. While Italians were among the last Europeans to head across the ocean, immigration was already an old story in the United States in 1888. Neither government aid nor benevolent societies existed for Italians arriving in New York. As the latest pilgrims to land there, they inherited the tenement slums and undesirable labor in mines, on plantations, or laying railway lines. Their Catholic faith ensured disapproval in schools and hospitals. Yet even in Catholic parishes these new immigrants found themselves outcasts. There were no Italian bishops and few Italian-speaking priests in the U.S., and these immigrants found no welcome in the Church.

With all this in mind, Pope Leo's words to Mother Cabrini were simple: "Not to the East, but to the West."[9] After this meeting, Cabrini never mentioned China again. In 1889, six plucky Missionary Sisters of the Sacred Heart accompanied Mother Cabrini onto a ship bound for New York. What awaited them on their arrival is a familiar refrain in the lives of U.S. saints. No arrangements had been made for the sisters, so they went to the same slums that housed their new parishioners and endured the misery firsthand. Deprivation and discomfort were acceptable terms, but lack of hygiene was something convent life would not abide. Vermin made sleep impossible. Worse, in touring the school intended for them the next day, the sisters found it in bad repair and unusable. No financial aid would be forthcoming from the archbishop, nor from the poor immigrants, nor even from established Italians, who quite emphatically separated themselves from their incoming compatriots.

When Mother Cabrini met with Archbishop Michael Corrigan the next day, he bluntly told her to go back to Italy; New York didn't need another orphanage. This shocking about-face is charitably explained only by Cabrini herself, who later suggested that pressure from anti-Italian lobbies may have forced the archbishop to retract his proposal. In any event, she replied immediately and firmly: "No, Your Grace, that is impossible. I have come here with the permission of the Holy See, and here I will remain."[10] Not many people spoke to an archbishop with such authority, and certainly fewer religious sisters. Corrigan gave this obstinate mother permission to open the school, but not the orphanage.

Permission was all Cabrini ever required to get a thing done. At once the sisters moved in with some accommodating Sisters of Charity, and opened a school in the Italian district at St. Joachim parish. They taught hundreds of children right in the church, using the pews as desks. They also made home visitations, climbing dark tenement stairs that led into dirty, dangerous passageways. Newspapers wrote up the story of thin, vulnerable sisters who spoke no English yet entered places police officers feared to go.

Cabrini found it invaluable to study the Italian district from this vantage point, noticing the effectiveness of the Protestant Five Points Mission that attracted her fellow citizens into its ranks. Protestant evangelists offered not just church, but schools, health care, and orphanages. Cabrini realized her sisters would succeed only if they responded to the needs of immigrants in a holistic way.

While the archbishop continued his campaign of refusals, the influential Countess di Cesnola championed the cause of an orphanage and underwrote the enterprise with donations she procured from other women friendly to the idea. Cabrini found a building in the right neighborhood that could serve as both convent and orphanage, but it was not an ideal facility. Windows didn't shut, the door would not lock, the stove didn't work, grime and insects abounded, and there was no room for a chapel.

The sisters prayed before the fireplace and made do. Neighborhood children rescued the mission, bringing lettuce, lemons, ice, a hand mirror—whatever they had—to the sisters. A Protestant girl supplied a Madonna statue and candles. The schoolchildren often followed the sisters home and stayed with them rather than return to dim rooms where their working parents would not be waiting for them. For her part, Cabrini counted every hour training the children as a means of catechizing the parents also. To her mind, the New York mission was a success.

Cabrini returned to Italy, but she was back in the U.S. a year later to complete the purchase of a Jesuit novitiate house, Manresa, two hours from New York City. The property was exquisite, but the Jesuits were willing to let it go cheaply because there was no fresh water supply. Once they sold it to Mother Cabrini, of course, she found water and opened her own U.S. novitiate.

The miraculous became mundane in Cabrini's world. A year earlier in Codogno, she had stopped a fire from spreading to her orphanage by making the sign of the cross over it with her one prized possession: a reliquary of forty-two "saint companions" that traveled with her everywhere. Cabrini put her confidence in St. Paul's declaration to the Philippians: "I can do all things through him who strengthens me" (4:13). This was, in her mind, an entirely practical method. If God intended a thing done, it would get done.

The forces of nature appeared to bow to Mother Cabrini's divinely appointed mission. But those miracles seem almost old-school compared with others: banks and ministers of finance also bent like twigs in her path. She entered many countries—the U.S., Nicaragua, Costa Rica, Brazil, Argentina, Panama—and somehow managed, as a foreigner and female with virtually no collateral, to procure loans from officers without sharing a common language. She had the same effect on unsympathetic cardinals as she did on Jewish landlords, hostile Freemasons, anti-Catholic property owners, and politicians bent on keeping both Catholics and Italian immigrants disenfranchised. Cabrini anticipated obstacles in each transaction; she also expected the Sacred Heart of Jesus to melt them like wax. Her faith was uncanny, and relentlessly rewarded.

Arriving in New Orleans in 1892, at the end of her South American mission, she learned that eleven Sicilians had been lynched in that city the year before. The friendly Bishop Francis Janssens asked her to stay for Easter; Cabrini essentially stayed for good, planting a house of sisters in the French Quarter. The sisters began in a tenement complex on St. Philip Street shared with twenty mostly Negro and mulatto families. Soon they had bought the whole building and attracted so much Catholic traffic that a local Italian priest moved closer to the sisters and turned their chapel into a virtual parish. The bishop was such a frequent visitor, he didn't bother to ring the bell.

Back in New York, Mother Cabrini was asked to assume responsibility for a hospital begun by another community that had relinquished its control after four months. She was reluctant to consider the idea for the usual reason: while schools could be managed internally by the Institute, administering a hospital required considerable external support. Then Cabrini had a dream in which the Blessed Virgin Mary was making up sickbeds, informing her: "I am doing what you do not want to do." Needless to say, ten sisters of the Institute took over the hospital at once.[11]

Cabrini soon discovered the hospital was up to its rafters in debt. This was commonly the case. U.S. hospitals routinely failed in that century. Cabrini's hospitals, however, would not fail; heaven orchestrated their necessity. She quickly closed that location and opened another in which the sisters would both live and tend to patients. The new hospital had no gas; water had to be carried in from a local restaurant, as did food. The patients had beds while the sisters slept on the floor. All were admitted without charge, and still the new Columbus Hospital stayed afloat. Doctors came and offered their services. Patients were served wine and pasta and were cared for in their native language. Recovery rates under these circumstances were unusually good. The Missionary Sisters were now officially in the health care business.

By 1892, the Institute had two hundred sisters in fourteen houses worldwide. Cabrini traveled the triangle from Italy to the United States to South America regularly. Schools remained the primary mission, especially the teachers' school in Rome. Without the education of the heart, Cabrini believed, charity would find no home in the world. Raising up teachers who imbued Gospel charity was paramount, and Cabrini wrote warm letters to her teachers annually, the last letter arriving in many teachers' hands a month after she died.

As the Institute spread around the western hemisphere, the need for linguistically versatile teachers became clear. In Cabrini fashion, this meant opening schools in Spain and France for her sisters' training, which she did before the close of the nineteenth century. As usual, clerics in Paris dismissed her and finances were unobtainable—and Cabrini made it happen anyway. Everyone got on board with her vision in the end.

The woman who was supposed to have died a decade earlier was still in full motion when the new century began. Back in the States, Mother Cabrini answered every invitation, opening schools in Chicago, Newark, and Scranton, Pennsylvania. Scranton was particularly important: it opened her eyes to the plight of Italian miners and led Cabrini's sisters to Denver as well, to assist the mining communities there. The sisters descended into mine shafts to bring comfort to men who rarely saw the sun or heard a gentle word. Where the Italians were, the Institute went. Even in prisons the sisters were there, reading letters to the illiterate, praying with the desperate, advocating for the wrongly sentenced.

By now, the name Cabrini spoke volumes in civic, social, and ecclesiastical circles. When Mother Cabrini came to town, she got a little more cooperation. Even in Rome, whenever she returned to visit with her great friend, Pope Leo XIII, he dispensed her from the ritual genuflections, exclaiming: "Come, come, Mother Cabrini; you have the spirit of God. Carry it to the whole world."[12] During one of Cabrini's critical seasons of illness, when death seemed inevitable, Pope Leo kept an eye on her condition from afar. After she recovered, he sent a basket of oranges from the Vatican orchards to celebrate her continued mission.

During the yellow fever epidemic of 1905, the New Orleans sisters tended the dying and took in orphans when necessary, locating relatives when possible even if it meant returning the children to Italy. Health officials, spread thinly through the city, learned to work with the sisters, sending them wagons of medicines and disinfectants. The bishop himself died of the fever, but not a single sister of the Institute got sick.

In twenty-five years, the Institute grew to almost one thousand women in fifty houses, caring for five thousand children in schools and orphanages, untold numbers of the sick in hospitals, and some ninety thousand immigrants served. All this happened through the driving vision of one chronically infirm woman who operated without resources and generally began with no more than a nod of encouragement.

Mother Cabrini could be found sweeping the floors of a new foundation until her hands were raw or stirring the kitchen polenta pot like somebody's *Nonna*. The next moment she would be dismissing dishonest contractors at a building site and taking over their work herself, as she had to do during the construction of the new Columbus Hospital in Chicago. It is hard to supply transitions in tracing the activities of Mother Cabrini, perhaps because there were none. She was here and there, doing this and that, but always with warmth, humor, passion, and an unassailable authority.

In 1905, the same year she opened a hospital in Chicago, Cabrini visited Los Angeles for the first time. There were only 150,000 people in Los Angeles then, and electric cars connected the city to the ocean. Every valley seemed like a natural sanitarium to her. She imagined any illness might be cured by those who breathed that wonderful air day and night. She quickly opened another foundation. She also extended the ministry of the Institute for the first time to Mexican immigrants there, who faced the same challenges as did her beloved Italians. Four years later, while reorganizing her institutions in Seattle, Cabrini gave herself more intimately to the country that had embraced her mission so completely, becoming a U.S. citizen at last.

At sixty, Mother Cabrini felt ready to retire. She wanted to take the time left to write down some thoughts for her sisters, but instead they enthusiastically elected her Mother Superior for life. She renounced the dream of rest and kept going. After another long illness in Italy in 1911, Cabrini determined to visit her foundations in the U.S. one more time.

It was a fateful choice. The Great War began, which made a return to Europe impossible, so she remained in her adopted country. Back and forth, from New York to Seattle and everywhere in between, Cabrini continued to visit old foundations and start new ones. By 1916 she was in great pain, leaning on a cane and often bedridden, her heart and lungs weakened by the old malarial microbes. But the woman who saw time as money to barter for eternity wasn't about to stop until heaven retired her. She died in Chicago in 1917, preparing Christmas candy for local children, slipping away as graciously as she had lived.

Frances Cabrini had seen what few people of her generation could expect to see. She had marveled at sea birds, icebergs, dolphins, and the mountains and valleys of ocean waves. She had glimpsed "fish called sharks, that eat people,"[13] and was enchanted by palm trees, Niagara Falls, "the giants of the vegetable kingdom" in California,[14] the Southwest deserts, and the Grand Canyon. She viewed an aurora borealis, described the Azores as "a piece of the sky dropped in the middle of the Atlantic,"[15] and rejoiced at a moon that seemed "like a huge frittata."[16] She saw active volcanoes and felt earthquakes. And everywhere Cabrini went, she sensed above all the immensity and omnipotence of God. Best of all, she wrote home about it so that generations more might share her vision of the universe.

In a meditative letter about the Mother of God, composed on shipboard, Cabrini once wrote: "Mary lived more in God than in herself. She was where she loved, more than where she lived."[17] The same could be said of Frances Xavier Cabrini.

Today

The Missionary Sisters of the Sacred Heart of Jesus went to China (1926), Australia (1948), and operate today in sixteen countries. Along with their other ministries, Cabrini Immigrant Services supplies language assistance, health care, and advocacy for newcomers to the U.S. Lay associates also assist today in their education of the heart. The National Shrine of Saint Frances Xavier Cabrini is located in Chicago, but two other significant shrines can be found in Golden, Colorado, and in northern Manhattan, where her body rests.

Timeline

1850:	Maria Francesca Cabrini born at Sant'Angelo Lodigiano in Lombardy, Italy, on July 15
1861:	House of Savoy unites most Italian city-states under its rule
1868:	Cabrini earns teacher's diploma
1880:	Cabrini founds Missionaries of the Sacred Heart
1887:	Cabrini goes to Rome to open a school and receive pontifical approval
1889:	Cabrini sails to New York the first time
1890s:	Cabrini begins South American missions
1898-1899:	Cabrini opens language schools in Paris and Madrid
1902-1906:	Institutions opened in Chicago, Scranton, Newark, Denver, and Seattle
1905:	Mission extended to Mexican immigrants in Los Angeles
1909:	Cabrini becomes a U.S. citizen in Seattle
1914:	World War I begins
1917:	Cabrini dies in Chicago, December 22, of malarial complications at age sixty-seven

12] Katharine (Catherine Mary) Drexel
(1858–1955)
America's Promise Keeper
Feast: March 3. Venerable: 1987. Beatified: 1988. Canonized: 2000.

I am, and have always been, one of the happiest women in the world.[1]

She had not left her bed the last five years of her life; you would think the world would have forgotten her. Yet thousands turned out to see the coffin bearing the body of a ninety-six-year-old woman carried by six men: two white, two black, two Native American. A man held up his child to give him a better view: "Take a look at the nun, son. Some day you can say that you looked upon a saint."[2] Those who knew her already considered her a saint. The press called her other things: "The Philadelphia heiress." "The Millionaire Nun." For Mother Katharine Drexel, time literally *was* money. Every moment she breathed was worth a fortune to the most forgotten people of America.

At her death, five hundred Sisters of the Blessed Sacrament, forty-eight elementary schools, twelve high schools, and one boundary-shattering college testified that Katharine Drexel had been a very busy woman. Hers was a unique kind of American success story, one that could be titled "The Checkbook and the Church." Her life proved that, when it comes to getting things done in this world, it often really is about the money. What makes Katharine a virtual patron saint of the One Percent is that she demonstrated how deftly rich folks can slip through the eye of the needle with room to spare. All they have to do is use their superior resources to the right ends.

Born at the brink of the Civil War, and dying just before the civil rights movement of another century, Catherine Mary Drexel inhabited an era given to much denial and little protest of great American injustices. The government had driven Native American tribes westward since the Indian Removal Act thirty years earlier, breaking faith with them at every step. Most Americans east of the Mississippi had forgotten—or wanted to forget—that the first Americans existed. A senator protesting government aid to those serving on the reservations publically framed the issue as many privately did: "These missionaries are merely presiding at the deathbed of a vanishing race."[3]

Kate Drexel was five years old in 1863, when Lincoln issued the Emancipation Proclamation. Her generation witnessed the next round of promises made and broken with another race of people caught in the crossfire of the European New World adventure. Northerners like the Drexels could afford not to think too much about these matters. Wealth can be a wonderful insulator from much of the world's hurt.

The first Francis Drexel came to America from the Austrian Tyrol in 1817. He was not rich, but hoped to make a quick killing as a portrait artist before returning home. Instead he married into one of Philadelphia's oldest families and had a half dozen children. Few things focus a breadwinner like a multiplication of mouths to feed. Drexel tried his hand at several businesses but made some enemies, one in particular within the family of his well-connected in-laws, which crushed his chances for success in Philadelphia.

Drexel headed to Mexico to restart his portrait business. That put him in the right place at the right time when President Andrew Jackson withdrew federal support from the Bank of the United States in 1835. Financial panic gripped the nation as banks slammed their doors, with consequences rippling out for citizens across the states—including foundresses with cash flow problems like Philippine Duchesne in Missouri. Suddenly, foreign currency looked pretty good. Drexel had the business acumen to reinvent himself as a broker overnight, setting up a currency trading business in the river port city of Louisville, Kentucky. In time he moved the operation to Philadelphia, making a great American fortune in the process.

Drexel's sons, Francis and Anthony, took over the business in 1863. Anthony was a financial genius with personal ties to Ulysses S. Grant. Anthony also left the Catholic Church when he married an Episcopalian. Both of these moves were good for business. Many prominent Philadelphia Catholics exited the Church after Bishop John Neumann won the battle over parish lay trusteeism in the civil courts. Anthony's brother Francis had been as heated about the issue as their late father but later reconciled with the Church, sending his considerable donations toward the archdiocese's many charities.

The Drexel firm underwrote finances for government, railroads, and corporate securities. As business soared, Francis married Hannah Jane Langstroth, and they had two children together, Elizabeth and Catherine Mary. Hannah Jane did not survive childbirth the second time. At a loss after her death, Francis sent the infant and toddler to live with his brother's family.

Fifteen months later Francis married again, this time to Emma Bouvier. Among the descendants of her family line would be Jacqueline Bouvier, wife of John F. Kennedy, the first Catholic President. Establishing a residence in center-city Philadelphia, Francis was glad to fetch his daughters from Anthony and bring them home.

Emma was never a "stepmother," Katharine later insisted. Emma showed no preference between the girls she inherited and Louise, who was born later to her and Francis. Nor did these sisters ever make distinctions, calling themselves the All-Three in later affectionate letters. This trinity of siblings may deserve an equal share in the canonization of the middle sister; Katharine always considered Louise the special saint among them.

Emma set up an oratory in the family home. She also spent her days with a project she called "the Dorcas," after the biblical woman of charity who appears in chapter nine of the Acts of the Apostles. The Dorcas involved assistance to the hundreds who gathered three days a week at the family's back gate. Mrs. Drexel wasn't one to simply hand out sandwiches. She hired a full-time social worker (before there was such a thing) to visit tenements and assess needs. Being nobody's fool, Emma also kept careful track as to who got what. Mr. Drexel, meanwhile, sat on every charitable board sponsored by the archdiocese and was a major contributor. Katharine later imitated her mother's attention to detail and her father's administrative thoroughness.

There is nothing new about people of means writing big checks to charitable organizations. Today, tax breaks make that advantageous. In the nineteenth century, the benefits were mostly prestigious. For the Drexels, a strong undercurrent of faith motivated their choices. They didn't wave their checkbook at social problems to assuage upper-class guilt. They were a believing family with sincere convictions as to their responsibilities toward the less fortunate.

Make no mistake: The Drexel girls lived privileged lives. Kate never attended school but was instructed at home by governesses. The family enjoyed a summer home in Torresdale, outside of Philadelphia, seventy acres the Drexels called St. Michel. When the archbishop visited, he celebrated Mass in their oratory. When they went abroad to Europe, papal audiences were included.

It was during the summers at St. Michel that young Kate encountered Father James O'Connor at the local parish. O'Connor became the spiritual guide of her discernment years. When he was named bishop to the Nebraska Territory in 1876—overseeing Nebraska, Wyoming, Montana, the Dakotas, and parts of Missouri—they maintained their relationship through letters. O'Connor's frontier appointment gave Kate a window onto a world she might otherwise have missed. Train travel had just opened the West. The Great Sioux War, including Custer's Last Stand, was recent news in O'Connor's territory. By contrast, Kate's comfortable Philadelphia bubble had kept her interests fairly parochial.

Kate had wrestled with her life's direction since childhood. She had a great devotion to the Blessed Sacrament and wanted to join the Carmelites mostly because they enjoyed the rare permission to receive communion daily rather than three times weekly like other religious. In his wisdom, O'Connor discouraged this course for an inexperienced daughter of wealth and advised her to pray about her path.

Kate, however, had practiced logical debate since an early childhood essay entitled "The Pros and Cons of Chicken-pox." In 1883 she drew up such a list concerning religious life for O'Connor. The pros for entering the convent were predictably pious: the right answers a dutiful student supplies. Her cons were more self-revealing: being away from her family made her homesick. She felt too proud to obey a superior—especially if the superior was "stupid." A life of luxury had not prepared her for privation, and she feared boredom. The most amusing note was number two on the list: "I hate community life. I should think it maddening to come in constant contact with many different old maidish dispositions. I hate never to be alone."[4]

While Kate hammered out her future, so did her father. Emma Drexel had died of cancer in 1882. Her death left Francis with three female heirs to protect from fortune hunters. He devised the ultimate firewall for the Drexel fortune. The inheritance would be split three ways and provide only annual income, not a lump sum. A child of his daughters could inherit the family money, but not a spouse. If one of the sisters died without children, her portion automatically reverted to the remaining sisters. These were fateful decisions in ways Francis could not have imagined.

Emma's death affected her daughters in diverse ways. Elizabeth resolved to marry and to involve herself in charities like her mother. Kate determined to leave the world and enter a cloister, despite her mentor's protestations. Louise had a severe nervous collapse, the first of many.

Drexel business required a westbound tour the following year. Francis engaged a private car on a train and took his daughters with him. Kate had no idea she would cross the United States many more times, but never in such comfort. On the far side of the adventure, in Tacoma, Washington, they met a missionary working among the Indians. His poor chapel had no statuary, so Kate offered to send him an image of its patron, Our Lady of Grace. It was her first gift to the missions, paid with the first check she ever wrote against a new monthly allowance. Kate had been interested in the native peoples for years, thanks to her friendship with O'Connor. But the investment had been intellectual and spiritual until now.

Money can purchase many things, but not immortality. In 1885, Francis Drexel caught a cold, which turned to pleurisy. He died of a heart attack weeks later. At his death, Francis was worth $15.5 million, a tithe of which went to his charities at once. The remaining $14 million belonged to his daughters. Overnight Elizabeth, Katharine, and Louise were the richest women in Philadelphia, and possibly the country. They were twenty-nine, twenty-six, and twenty-one years old, respectively.

Being Drexels, the sisters immediately applied themselves to charity, starting with a memorial to their father. A residential training school to assist orphans toward attaining a livelihood seemed right. Elizabeth established St. Francis de Sales Industrial School toward that end. Louise developed her concern for the welfare of the post-Civil War black community into "a school for Negro boys" named St. Emma's after her mother. Katharine complemented Louise's efforts with a school for Negro girls adjacent to the property in Maryland, which went by the name Rock Castle. But there was no doubt her special interest lay in the Indian missions to the West.

Opportunity would soon knock. Two priests came to call in Philadelphia, Benedictine Bishop Martin Marty of the Dakota Territory and Father Joseph Stephan of the Bureau of Catholic Indian Missions. They were anxious for Katharine to appreciate what her involvement could accomplish. She gave them five hundred dollars at this initial contact—and lifelong dedication to their cause.

Katharine was coming to terms with the Indian question from within its complicated history. Native tribes forced westward were ill-prepared for the lands they now inhabited and ill-equipped to join a society powered by technical advancement and all-important literacy. In 1870, President Grant had adopted a peace policy through which agencies assisting Indians were turned over to religious denominations with historical ties to each tribe. The government supplied contracts with financial aid attached. The religious groups built facilities and staffed them.

In the late nineteenth century, the boarding school concept seemed the most humane way to incorporate native peoples into the benefits of American society. Now the idea is viewed as cultural genocide and a basic denial of parental rights, but then it appeared the best solution to a problematic legacy. As Grant stated, it was better to Christianize the Indians than to kill them. Of the seventy-two service agencies in question, the Catholic bishops expected to be awarded thirty-eight contracts, since they had principal contact with those tribes.

Catholic missionaries were awarded only eight contracts, however, proportionate to their presence in the population, and eighty thousand Catholic Indians were given over to Protestant supervision. As usual, no one asked the tribes what they wanted. A leader of the Osage community protested: "Religion among the whites is a matter of conscience and voluntary choice.... It is so throughout all Christendom; and why should it not be so among the Osages? Give us, we beseech you, our choice in this matter."[5] By 1881, the situation was corrected: all denominations were granted equal access to the reservations.

Access was one thing, finances another, and personnel a third factor in the effort. American Catholicism of the era was not noted for evangelization. Absorbing immigrants by the millions, bishops had little attention or resources for anything else, and so bishops in Indian Territory were on their own.

The Bureau of Catholic Indian Missions was established in 1874 to coordinate efforts nationwide. When the Third Plenary Council of Baltimore in 1884 included Indian and Negro missions on the agenda, the bishops most affected by the issues considered a lack of personnel the biggest obstacle to their work. Present clergy and religious were stretched to the breaking point dealing with the European influx.

As Katharine Drexel started underwriting the Indian missions, up to the first million dollars, Bishop O'Connor continued to discourage her interest in the cloister. Her vow of poverty would result in the loss of a great opportunity for the missions. Her mother Emma had been of the same opinion: women of means had an obligation to remain "in the world" to use their privilege for the underprivileged. Katharine's job, the bishop assured her, was to be Christ's steward: "Much of the good you will thus be able to do in the world, you would not be free to perform in religion."[6] O'Connor insisted Katharine had the means, the brains, and the freedom of action necessary to do great good. In religious life, her energies would be dominated by others. Better to fund a novitiate for women training for native missions than for her to shuffle off to a secure obscurity.

The Drexel sisters went to Europe again in 1886. During the

inevitable papal audience, Katharine got a little demonstrative, kneeling at the feet of Pope Leo XIII and pleading for him to send missionaries to help Bishop O'Connor's Indians. She was horrified when the pope directed the matter back to her: "Why not, my child, yourself become a missionary?"[7] As already noted, this pope also befriended another female missionary, Frances Cabrini. Leo XIII had no qualms about what a passionate woman might accomplish.

Katharine Drexel had been trapped by her ostentatious gesture. Dissolved was the dream of slipping away to a cloister. Back home, Bishop O'Connor regarded this papal suggestion as a mandate. Yet the Drexel fortune still hung in the balance. O'Connor and his missionary friend Father Stephan came up with the perfect solution: Kate should found her own order, and draw an exceptional exemption from the poverty vow.

It would take another two years for Katharine to be convinced. These were busy years, as the sisters went on a fact-finding tour of Indian country with O'Connor and Stephan. They traveled on trains until they ran out of rails, then went farther by coach, buckboard, and horseback. They visited foundations Katharine had already established, and met personalities like Red Cloud, a chief of the Sioux.

Tribal members expressed thanks that she had built them a home for the "Big Prayer"—the Indian term for Mass. Along the way, Katharine became godmother for a Chippewa boy named William. What became apparent was this; tribal chiefs wanted what the government had promised since 1868 but had failed to provide: the advantages of an education for their children. Gesturing toward the cemetery, one chief said simply, "It is the wish of those who now sleep out there, and it is even more our wish."[8]

Constructing schools was easy. Staffing them was nearly impossible. The Drexel sisters pledged thirty thousand dollars to the Sisters of St. Francis of Philadelphia to staff ten missions. Over the years Katharine would employ every means of securing teachers: funding other religious orders, paying lay teachers, and eventually, sending her own uniquely prepared religious.

In 1888, Louise was engaged to Edward Morrell, a lawyer who would become a valuable ally in Congress for Drexel causes. Ned raised the issue of the Negro vote a half-century before Americans were prepared to consider it. Elizabeth had also privately reached an understanding with Walter George Smith, another lawyer, who invested himself in the corporate ministries of the "All-Three."

Katharine could postpone her own future no longer. O'Connor assured her that he was certain of no vocation more than hers, not even his own. She made arrangements to enter the novitiate of the Sisters of Mercy in Pittsburgh with the peculiar goal of learning how to be a sister and a foundress simultaneously.

The Pittsburgh plan was not exactly pulled out of a hat. Katharine had considered a Philadelphia order like the Franciscan Sisters Bishop Neumann had founded. But O'Connor's brother was the Bishop of Pittsburgh, and he had brought the Mercy Sisters to the States and vouched for their spirit.

What was less certain was where the new order should be established once Katharine's preparation was complete. Bishop Marty opted for up north with him in Sioux Falls. Father Stephan imagined her near the Bureau of Catholic Indian Missions, which he directed in Washington, D.C., or perhaps in Banning, California, where she had recently opened a school and would be closer to Southwest tribes. Her spiritual director, as always, had the most powerful hand in the matter: O'Connor wanted her in Philadelphia, where she could attract more postulants.

A supportive bishop was vital, and Archbishop Patrick Ryan of Philadelphia was a Drexel ally and supporter of missionaries like Frances Cabrini as well. Ned Morrell, by then Louise's husband, purchased some property just north of Drexel territory at St. Michel for the new community.

During her novitiate, Katharine's sisters monitored her missions while she focused on the enormous task ahead of her. She was to be the founder of "the Sisters of the Blessed Sacrament for Indians and Colored People"—rather a tall order for the 1890s. But it was not unheard of to found a race-specific ministry. The white Mill Hill fathers, later called Josephites, had won permission to work exclusively with freed slaves. Two communities of women, the Oblate Sisters of Providence started by Elizabeth Lange in 1829 and the Sisters of the Holy Family founded by Henriette Delille in 1842, were exclusively comprised of black women working within the black community.

No religious orders had been founded to work with Native Americans, nor to include them. The needs of six hundred thousand Indians might be unfairly compared with the seven million African Americans of Katharine's generation. But she optimistically viewed her mission to native peoples as a twenty-five-year plan that would end along with the reservation system. She couldn't have imagined that the "Colored" mission would meet its significant game-changer first, when Brown met the Board of Education in Topeka, Kansas, in 1954.

How did Katharine envision her task? It wasn't just a matter of opening schools for people of color across America. Schools were fundamental; so was the care of orphans and attention to the sick. Home visitations were vital, to know the people and their needs firsthand, as Emma Drexel had with her Dorcas project. Prison visitation and instruction was part of the plan, as well as shelter for women in distressful situations. Her order would also aid priests, religious, and others engaged in the work. The organization would be comprehensive and well-managed; after all, Katharine was her father's daughter.

Katharine wasn't dogmatic about the scope of her concerns. When Father Damien de Veuster wrote her about his needs in Molokai, the Drexel sisters responded. In her lifetime Katharine received a medal of honor from the President of Haiti. After her death, letters of gratitude came from missionaries in Uganda, British Honduras, and Canada.

Katharine didn't regard herself as sole proprietor of the task ahead. She recommended that the U.S. bishops organize an annual collection for Black and Indian missions. She felt Catholics everywhere had to take these missions to heart. The American soul was endangered by the neglect of its spurned peoples. So much national attention was given to massacres by Indians, but no one remembered the massacres *of* Indians: of Conestoga near Philadelphia in 1763 or the killing of peaceful Cheyenne in Colorado in 1864.

Archbishop Ryan underscored this message when addressing his fellow bishops at the Second Plenary Council of Baltimore: "I believe that Negro slavery and the unjust treatment of the Indians are the two great blots on American civilization.... I feel that in the Church also, the most reasonable cause for regret in the past century is the fact that more could have been done for these dependent classes. Let us now come in the name of God and resolve to make reparations."[9]

The great venture nearly derailed before Katharine finished her novitiate; in 1890, Bishop O'Connor was dying. He returned to Pittsburgh to be near his brother and to benefit from the care of the Mercy Sisters. Katharine still had great need of her spiritual advisor, to settle questions such as whether women of color should be welcomed into the order. Louise and Katharine both were in favor of it, but priests they consulted said a "colored third order" was the most that could be considered.

Elizabeth scoffed that color-coding religious life was plain ridiculous, but O'Connor persuaded Katharine to let the idea of a mixed-race community go. The Civil War was mere decades in the past. The Jim Crow South forbid living quarters shared by different races. Even boarding schools for black children run by white nuns pressed the law to the breaking point. What would it mean for community life?

Bishop O'Connor's death left Katharine reeling. This community had been his idea all along; how was she to found it without him? Archbishop Ryan visited Katharine in Pittsburgh after O'Connor's funeral. "I can't go on," she blurted out. Ryan knew her well enough to know what had to be said, and he said it: "If I share the burden with you, if I help you, can you go on?"[10] His offer worked. She completed her novitiate and was ready to begin.

However, the year remained one of loss and misery. Elizabeth returned from her honeymoon sick and died with her unborn child. Her husband, Walter George Smith, would never remarry. A devastated Louise had a relapse. And silently, beneath the tragedy, the inheritance was redistributed between the two remaining sisters. They pledged to maintain Elizabeth's school as well as to pursue their own works.

The year 1890 also saw a national tragedy at Wounded Knee Creek on the Pine Ridge Reservation in South Dakota, where an "uprising" was grossly mishandled. Federal troops slaughtered hundreds of men, women, and children, including the great Chief Sitting Bull. The Franciscan Sisters who staffed Katharine's school at Pine Ridge were only spared violent reprisal through the personal protection of Chief Red Cloud, befriended earlier. The need for a deep commitment to promise-keeping between U.S. citizens and the first Americans was never more obvious.

Mother Katharine Drexel founded her community with fourteen members the following year. The federal contract system assisting agencies involved with Indian tribes, now two decades old, was fraying, its budget diminishing every year under President Harrison's administration. Wherever the cuts landed, Mother Katharine picked up the shortfall. She was anxious to rush her own sisters to the reservations; Archbishop Ryan had to order her under obedience to wait until they had received a full formation and preparation for such challenging work. Katharine resigned herself to finding and funding other religious personnel for the work: Josephites, Benedictines, Jesuits, Franciscans, Sisters of Charity, even Protestant lay staff.

The new Sisters of the Blessed Sacrament received a comprehensive education from Drexel University in Philadelphia, founded by Katharine's uncle Anthony. It was the only coeducational school in the city. The sisters studied academics as well as domestic sciences for their missions: milking a cow, sewing, shoe making. The community was made aware of the opposition they would endure at the opening of their first convent—with a bomb threat. Not everyone saw the education of Indian and black children as a desirable goal. Mother Katharine made it a practice to insure all of her buildings immediately.

The question of race within her ranks continued to be raised. An early applicant from the Seneca tribe was maintained as a "guest" of the order until other arrangements could be made. Eventually, she did make her profession as a Blessed Sacrament Sister. In 1893 Mother Matilda Beasley, founder of a Third Order of black Franciscans, asked to merge her group with Mother Katharine's, as her order could no longer sustain itself. Katharine gave financial help but, in the end, a southern bishop suppressed the order and Mother Matilda returned to the lay state.

Katharine's sensitivity to existing black religious communities and white orders working with black churches kept her from sending her sisters to the South for years. She didn't want to compete with their schools or in recruitment of candidates. Instead, she limited her involvement to funding existing communities and steering potential candidates to them.

Personally, Katharine chafed at preserving an all-white order to work with people of color. She heard the arguments of those in the field who assured her that black candidates would discourage white ones from entering. More compelling were debates about community discipline risking the appearance of being racially motivated, or that some works couldn't be undertaken at all because of civil laws against mixing races in the South. An integrated community had been attempted by the Sisters of the Presentation in New Orleans and suppressed. Mother Katharine had to resign herself to wait for another generation. In the meantime, she subsidized the work of black leaders like Augustus Tolton, a former slave and the first black Roman Catholic priest ordained in the United States, to the tune of thirty thousand dollars over the years.

Blessed Sacrament Sisters began staffing their own schools in 1894. The first was St. Catherine's in Santa Fe, New Mexico, among the Pueblo Indians. Katharine established six more schools in the Southwest, including St. Michael's in Navajo country; the tribe was so fearful of delivering their children to the white nuns that parents camped on the grounds for weeks until they were sure their children were not in danger. (Because of the great distances involved in the Southwest ministries, Katharine would later make a practical concession against simplicity of lifestyle by purchasing the sisters in New Mexico a car in 1935.)

By the end of the nineteenth century, Katharine was already invested, in one way or another, in twenty-six dioceses. She had also given one hundred thousand dollars to various projects in the South, always being creative about working for justice. For example, she gave aid to white churches on the contingency that they would make pews for blacks available in the congregation, not in the customary upper gallery. Whereas the government partnered with her in Indian territory, no external funding contributed to her work with black Americans. Her school for black girls in Rock Castle supplied potential teachers for a much wider educational enterprise in the South. But they needed to advance in their studies, and there were so few places where that was possible.

Mother Katharine dealt with dozens of unusually cooperative bishops, compared with her predecessor foundresses. It helped that she was a born-and-bred American. She spoke the language, and with refinement and style. No doubt the Drexel brand also greased the wheels for her. The wise superior of the Mercy Sisters read the situation correctly when she advised Katharine to keep her name in religion. Many bishops treated Mother Katharine like a fairy godmother who could address all their needs with a wave of her pen: parishes, schools, staffing, funding. Her ability to solve problems seemed limitless.

But some things even a Drexel couldn't buy. The community rule continued to sprout unfathomable problems between Philadelphia and Rome. One day in 1907, as a perplexed Katharine pored over the latest drafts, a slight Italian woman showed up in her parlor. It was Mother Cabrini. While the two had not met before, the Blessed Sacrament Sisters had lent some hospitality to Cabrini's Sacred Hearts. Cabrini had come to express her gratitude. She left Katharine with some advice about how to deal with Rome: go there and settle the rule in person. "And don't come back until you can bring your approval with you." Mother Katharine took the advice.[11]

Archbishop Ryan, Katharine's second mentor, died in 1911. At fifty-three, she now knew how to proceed without an advisor. She bought properties for her schools by means of third-party transactions wherever the sellers wouldn't sell to a Catholic or to a white nun set on educating black children. Before 1912, the calls for assistance with the black mission had come from southern bishops; now they were coming from northern cities like Columbus, Chicago, New York, and Boston. The great African American migration from the South to the North had begun.

In 1912, Katharine Drexel touched her own mortality. During annual visitations to her communities out west, she became ill, first diagnosed with pneumonia, then typhoid fever. An irregular heartbeat was detected. Her doctor ordered her to slow down or risk jeopardizing her entire mission. Katharine always longed for a more hands-on role in the work of her order, but her sisters couldn't afford to lose her. Everything they accomplished—now also in Nashville, Atlanta, and Macon—depended on the peculiar terms of her father's will.

Mother Katharine had stayed out of New Orleans before 1915. This most historically Catholic of cities had plenty of religious, and Katharine didn't want to undercut their efforts. Then the elderly Archbishop Blenk reported to Mother Katharine that Southern University, the only state college open to black Catholics, had moved from New Orleans to Baton Rouge. He lamented: "Our poor colored get only the leftovers." Blenk felt New Orleans needed an excellent black high school to prepare students for his ultimate dream: "Perhaps some day a university for our colored Catholics."

Blenk must have known he was talking to the dream-maker. "First of all, a location," Mother replied, ever practical. The archbishop fired back: "Old Southern University is for sale." Katharine asked him to get her a price. "I already have one: $18,000," Blenk admitted.[12] Xavier University came to life almost overnight, starting with a high school and adding grades each year. It was the first and only black Catholic college in the United States, coeducational from the start and with an integrated faculty. At last, Katharine's schools would have all the qualified black teachers she needed.

As Xavier thrived, she opened twenty-four small rural schools across Louisiana staffed with Xavier graduates. Katharine built even where former schools had been burned down. Until *Brown v. Board of Education* integrated public education the year before she died, Katharine's schools met the need.

Mother Katharine developed bronchitis in 1917 and was confined to the convent infirmary. She longed to be in the chapel every hour of her slow convalescence. Ned Morrell constructed an interior bay window overlooking the chapel from her bed. It was his last kindness to his sister-in-law, as he died later that year.

Louise, never strong emotionally, relied on her sister's courage even more after her husband's death. The world seemed to be getting colder, meaner. A world war had begun abroad, and the Ku Klux Klan was busy at home. One of Katharine's projects was threatened in Beaumont, Texas; members of the Klan beat up a black parishioner to make their point clear. A cross was burned near a school in Pennsylvania. A pastor was forced out of his church in Louisiana for burying a black woman too close to white graves. Fights broke out in Catholic churches if a black child dipped his hand in the baptismal font before a white person.

Walter George Smith, Elizabeth's widower, recommended that Katharine do more public speaking. People would listen to her because she was the Millionaire Nun. They would come for the novelty, but encounter the challenge. Katharine learned to speak tough truths in her low, gentle voice. At Notre Dame she observed that only two Catholic colleges in the state admitted Negro students. She confronted audiences bluntly about the willingness to give money—but never justice—to the black community. She wrote to the press exposing a biased media policy: "You don't say 'white man slays two' but if it is a Negro, it is always mentioned."[13]

In 1930, Louise and Katharine together wrote to the Secretary of Labor in Washington, arguing for human rights: "Colored were the last hired and the first fired."[14] The Church didn't escape the Drexel truth machine. Arguing for more positive role models from the black community, Katharine joined ten other signatories petitioning U.S. bishops to include the Uganda martyrs and St. Peter Claver on the

Church calendar in all dioceses.

Requests kept coming in, and Katharine met them. The new head of the Indian Bureau needed help: Tekakwitha House was opened in Washington, D.C. A Benedictine priest in South Dakota needed personnel, not money. Katharine had none to spare but sent three sisters anyway.

The Drexel fortune took a hit in the Great Depression; thirty-five percent of it was lost. Inflation also shrank what the money could do. The stellar expansion of the Blessed Sacrament's missionary empire further tightened resources. Then the introduction of income taxes in 1921 cut Mother Katharine's income in half.

Her ever-useful brother-in-law Walter George Smith sought tax relief through Congress. Governor George Wharton Pepper of Pennsylvania introduced a bill advocating that anyone giving at least 90 percent of their income to charity should not have to pay income tax. Suspicion mounted that the law had been crafted for John D. Rockefeller. In fact, Katharine Drexel was the only person in America who benefited. Her brother-in-law died just after the law was enacted.

Katharine had 190 sisters and 80 lay teachers in her schools by 1930. But more were needed—a lot more. Louise advocated for a lay apostolate; the time had come for the laity of the Church to assume leadership. It was a forward-looking vision but yielded modest results. Catholics of the era were not ready to jump onto the justice bandwagon, nor had the hour of the laity arrived. The problem with the Drexels was that they had a bird's-eye view of where the world was going. Few could see what they did.

Spurred on by two politically minded brothers-in-law, and affected by the more open political climate of a new century, Katharine Drexel got political. Women had won the right to vote in 1920; Katharine had her sisters register in 1928. She threw her support behind the NAACP. In 1934, she read about the 5,068th lynching since 1882. She lobbied for an anti-lynching bill before Congress. It was defeated.

A heart attack slowed down Katharine further in 1934. Then there was another. She started to have occasional falls. A possible cerebral hemorrhage was suspected. Dilation of the heart and arterial trouble were certain. Her doctor insisted she limit both work and travel, asserting that she owed it to humanity to prolong her life.

"No one is necessary to do the work of God, Doctor. He could do all the work without any of us," Katharine noted. "I agree with you, Mother," her cardiologist said, "but ordinarily He does not."[15] She suffered small relapses for the next two years. After that, though Katharine lived another twenty years, she rarely left the motherhouse. Her ministry was her correspondence; always, she promised prayers and a check.

Confined to a wheelchair by 1937, Mother Katharine stayed connected to her missions by praying for each one daily as she looked through the bay window of the infirmary into the chapel: Alabama, Arizona, California, Georgia, Illinois, Indiana, Louisiana, Massachusetts, Mississippi, Missouri, Nebraska, New Mexico, New York, Ohio, Pennsylvania, South Dakota, Tennessee, Texas, Virginia, Washington, D.C. Another world war came and went. Katharine prayed for the soldiers on both sides, "and even Hitler and even myself."[16]

One day in 1945, Louise stopped in for her weekly visit, promising to come again as she left. But she died of a cerebral hemorrhage days later. The sisters feared to tell their Mother that her little sister and longest partner in the crusade against injustice was gone. Katharine struggled with the news: "It is not that I want anything different from what God wants, but I cannot believe that life is taken from me—I cannot."[17]

The Drexel inheritance now silently rearranged itself entirely behind Katharine, eighty-seven years old and quite frail. The estate Louise left was sparse: she had been selling off even heirloom family jewelry to finance her ministries. Katharine's income, however, doubled overnight. Totally bedridden, enduring heart attacks and strokes, even a mastectomy, Katharine survived another decade. She sometimes wandered into delirium, or perhaps visions. These were quiet years for her. New postulants who encountered their foundress remembered nothing but her smile. She spent the final five years in bed praying black rosary beads turned brown from use.

Mother Katharine lived long enough to see some dreams come true. When public schools were integrated by law in 1954, many of her schools were shuttered. The Blessed Sacrament Sisters received their first black postulant in 1952; she would be at the head of the order at Mother Katharine's canonization. Redemptorists in Rome, already working on the cause of Philadelphia's Bishop Neumann, would stay to work on Katharine Drexel's.

Most of the Blessed Sacrament schools had worked themselves to a break-even basis before Mother Katharine's death, anticipating the loss of funding. What was left of the Drexel money was dispersed at her last breath to Francis Drexel's original charities. The sisters received assistance from the Archdiocese of Philadelphia for another ten years, as well as from the Bureau of Catholic Indian Missions.

Overall Katharine Drexel had spent nearly twenty million dollars (worth $330 million in today's values) maintaining sixty missions as the conscience of the American church. But it wasn't just about the money. It was also, and fundamentally, about the dedication of three sisters to remember the people other Americans were prepared to forget.

Today

Headquartered in Bensalem, Pennsylvania, the Blessed Sacrament Sisters continue their interracial apostolate in thirteen states and Haiti. They actively oppose prejudice, racism, and oppression, and partner with others in works of justice and environmental responsibility. Their first school, St. Michael's in Santa Fe, is still in operation. Both Xavier University and the preparatory high school in New Orleans still thrive. The Mission Center and Shrine in Bensalem also contains the entombed remains of the saint.

Timeline

1830:	Indian Removal Act forces tribes westward
1858:	Catherine Mary Drexel born on November 26 in Philadelphia

1863:	Emancipation Proclamation issued by President Lincoln
1870:	Francis Drexel purchases St. Michel property in Torresdale
1883-1885:	Drexel's stepmother and father die, leave immense inheritance
1887:	Drexel meets Pope Leo XIII and receives mandate
1889:	Catholic University of America opens
1891:	Sisters of the Blessed Sacrament founded
1894::	First mission staffed by sisters in Santa Fe
1908:	U.S. Church removed from the Congregation of the Propaganda of the Faith
1925:	Xavier University in New Orleans opens
1955:	Drexel dies on March 3 in Cornwells Heights (Bensalem), at age ninety-six

Epilogue

What Does It Take to Be an American Saint?

The women and men profiled in this book are not cookie-cutter personalities. They inhabited different vantage points across four centuries and sometimes conformed to social and religious conventions typical of their generations. Some may seem outmoded in their thinking, and others remarkably modern in spirit. Yet there are constants that connect their stories and their striving. Here are ten shared traits to consider in defining the character of these saints:

Prayer. They were all rooted in prayer from their earliest years, especially the celebration of the Eucharist and the practice of contemplation. A fascination with heroic stories of holy people and their deeds and the strength of family faith also grounded many of these saints. The example of family members and access to committed priests and religious marked their early lives.

Obedience. Most of these saints were convinced that obedience was the first among virtues. This didn't imply a lockstep deference to any command, as frequent skirmishes with authorities made obvious. At the heart of virtuous obedience is the attitude of careful attention to the divine will. They listened for God to speak, and then they acted with confidence.

Humility. It was important to these saints to vanish from view, to "decrease" so that God could "increase" in the scheme of things. Many saints actively fought promotions. If obedience required embracing them, they found other ways to remain lowly: cleaning the outhouse, scrubbing floors, mending shoes.

Austerity. Simplicity of lifestyle was paramount, starting with freedom from possessions. Religious communities relieve their members of individual property but sometimes hold enough common wealth to blur the distinction. Not these saints. Even the richest among them, Katharine Drexel, was meticulous about living a genuine, personal, voluntary poverty.

Collaboration. There were no lone wolves among the holy ones. Whatever their personal gifts, they relied heavily on community and church structures wherever they went. Often they accepted the hospitality of other religious orders in new territory. Even the laywoman Kateri looked for a faith community to support her efforts and cooperated with clergy to accomplish her tasks.

Adventurous Spirit. Some of the saints were notably shy, but all showed a remarkable spirit in moving beyond natural limits and traditional roles to become extraordinary people. Many left their original countries, Kateri moved beyond her tribe, Seton beyond her given religion and social class, Drexel beyond her race. Women did what women were not "meant" to do. The healthy risked the realm of contagion.

Curiosity. It would be hard to be a saint without an eagerness to learn and grow. Some of the saints were avid readers, even scholars. Others, like Cabrini, reveled in new experiences and fresh cultures. Belgian peasant Damien found a deep affinity with native Hawaiians. The Jesuits became keen reporters of the anthropology of the Indian nations with which they engaged. As long as she was able, Drexel never made decisions without going on fact-finding missions first.

Flexibility. Sometimes we make the mistake of thinking that the orthodoxy of belief requires an unyielding method and perspective. The saints, grounded in Real Presence, became truly present to those whom they served. This made them pliant to situations even as they conformed readily to religious rule. They changed their minds. They even changed their hearts when necessary.

Steadfastness. Sainthood is no realm for quitters. Even after her bishop and her most capable administrator both returned to France in defeat, Philippine Duchesne remained at her post. Guérin faced down her bishop. Neumann fought anti-Catholics. Damien endured loneliness. Jogues lost his fingers, then returned to surrender his life.

Courage. The bottom line for these men and women is that they were fearless. Not that they didn't feel fear; in fact, they reported dread and anxiety regularly. But they laid every danger against the great treasure of their mission, and put fear aside. They trusted in God more than their doubts. They did what had to be done. And by the witness of their lives, they invite us to do the same.

Bibliography

For more information about the saints and beatified who appear in this book, please refer to the following titles:

BOOKS

Baldwin, Lou. *Saint Katharine Drexel: Apostle to the Oppressed.* Philadelphia: The Catholic Standard and Times, 2000.

Boever, Richard A., C.SS.R. *Saint John Neumann: His Writings and Spirituality.* Liguori, Mo.: Liguori, 2010.

Burton, Katherine. *The Eighth American Saint: The Life of Saint Mother Theodore Guerin, Foundress of the Sisters of Providence of Saint Mary-of-the-Woods, Indiana.* Chicago: ACTA, 2007.

———. *The Golden Door: The Life of Katharine Drexel.* New York: P. J. Kenedy & Sons, 1957.

Byerley, Fr. Timothy E. *Saint John Neumann, Wonder-Worker of Philadelphia: Recent Miracles 1961–1991.* Philadelphia: National Shrine of St. John Neumann, 1992.

Cabrini, Frances X. *To the Ends of the Earth: The Missionary Travels of Frances X. Cabrini.* Philippa Provenzano, M.S.C., trans. New York: Center for Migration Studies, 2001.

Callan, Louise, R.S.C.J. *Philippine Duchesne: Frontier Missionary of the Sacred Heart 1769–1852.* Abridged edition. Westminster, Md.: Newman, 1965. Reprinted by Society of the Sacred Heart, United States Province, 2002.

Celeste, Sr. Marie, S.C. *The Intimate Friendships of Elizabeth Ann Bayley Seton: First Native Born American Saint (1774–1821).* New York: Alba House, 1989.

Cholonec, Fr. Pierre, S.J. *Kateri Tekakwitha: The Iroquois Saint, With an Account of the Iroquois Martyrs.* Abbrev. ed. Merchantville, N.J.: Arx, 2012.

Curley, Michael J., C.SS.R. *Venerable: John Neumann C.SS.R.: Fourth Bishop of Philadelphia.* Philadelphia: Bishop John Neumann Center, 1952.

———. *Cheerful Ascetic: The Life of Francis Xavier Seelos, C.SS.R.* 2nd ed. New Orleans: The Redemptorists, Seelos Center, 2002.

Daws, Gavan. *Holy Man: Father Damien of Molokai.* Honolulu: University of Hawaii Press, 1973.

De Maria, Mother Saverio, M.S.C. *Mother Frances Xavier Cabrini.* Rose Basile Green, trans. Chicago: Missionary Sisters of the Sacred Heart of Jesus, 1984.

Dolan, Jay P. *The American Catholic Experience: A History from Colonial Times to the Present.* Garden City, N.Y.: Doubleday, 1985.

Ellis, John Tracy. *American Catholicism.* 2nd ed. Chicago: University of Chicago Press, 1969.

Galvin, James J., C.SS.R. *Saint John Neumann: Fourth Bishop of Philadelphia.* Baltimore: Helicon, 1977.

Glazier, Michael, and Thomas J. Shelley, editors. *The Encyclopedia of American Catholic History.* Collegeville, Minn.: Liturgical, 1997.

Greer, Allan. *Mohawk Saint: Catherine Tekakwitha and the Jesuits.* New York: Oxford University Press, 2005.

Hackel, Steven W. *Junípero Serra: California's Founding Father.* New York: Hill and Wang, 2013.

Hanley, Sr. Mary Laurence, O.S.F. and O. A. Bushnell. *Pilgrimage and Exile: Mother Marianne of Molokai.* Rev. ed. Honolulu: Mutual, 2009.

Jogues, Fr. Isaac, and John Gilmary Shea. *Narrative of a Captivity Among the Mohawk Indians, and a Description of New Netherland in 1642–3 (1856).* North Charleston, S.C.: CreateSpace, 2011.

Law, Anwei Skinsnes and Henry G. Law. *Father Damien…A Bit of Taro, A Piece of Fish, and A Glass of Water.* Seneca Falls, N.Y.: IDEA Center for the Voices of Humanity, 2009.

Melville, Annabelle M. *Elizabeth Bayley Seton: 1774–1821.* New York: Charles Scribner's Sons, 1951.

Mitchell, Penny Blaker. *Mother Theodore Guerin—Saint of God: A*

Woman for All Time. Saint Mary-of-the-Woods, Ind.: Sisters of Providence, 2006.

Mooney, Catherine M. *Philippine Duchesne: A Woman with the Poor*. Eugene, Oreg.: Wipf & Stock, 1990.

O'Brien, John A. *Saints of the American Wilderness: The Brave Lives and Holy Deaths of the Eight North American Martyrs*. Manchester, N.H.: Sophia Institute, 2004.

Neumann, John, C.SS.R. *The Autobiography of St. John Neumann, C.SS.R*. Alfred C. Rush, C.SS.R., trans. Boston: St. Paul, 1977.

Santa, Thomas M. *The Little Way of Faithfulness: A Life of Francis Xavier Seelos, C.SS.R.* New Orleans: The Redemptorists, Seelos Center, 2011.

VIDEOS

Damien. DVD. Directed by Nino J. Martin. San Francisco: Ignatius, 2006.

Molokai: The Story of Father Damien. DVD. Directed by Paul Cox. Worcester, Pa.: Vision Video, 2013.

An Uncommon Kindness: The Father Damien Story. DVD. Directed by Stephanie Castillo. Olena Media, 2006.

Notes

PART ONE
1. Antonio de Montesinos, quoted in Paul E. Pierson, *The Dynamics of Christian Mission: History through a Missiological Perspective* (Pasadena, Calif.: William Carey International University Press, 2009), p. 172.
2. John Tracy Ellis, *American Catholicism*, 2nd ed. (Chicago: University of Chicago Press, 1969), p. 151.
3. John Hughes, *The complete works of the Most Rev. John Hughes, Archbishop of New York: comprising his sermons, letters, lectures, speeches, etc*, vol. II (New York: Catholic Publication House, 1864), p. 715.
4. Ellis, p. 89.
5. Francis P. Kenrick, *Theologia moralis*, I, 257, as quoted in Ellis, p. 90.
6. Penny Blaker Mitchell, *Mother Theodore Guerin–Saint of God: A Woman for All Time* (Saint Mary-of-the-Woods, Ind.: Sisters of Providence, 2007), p. 102.

PART TWO
CHAPTER ONE
1. Georges-Émile Giguère, "Jogues, Isaac," *Dictionary of Canadian Biography*, vol. 1, University of Toronto/Université Laval, accessed October 26, 2013, http://www.biographi.ca/en/bio/jogues_isaac_1E.html.
2. Pope Paul VI, *Allocution to the 32nd General Congregation*, 1975, as quoted in Jesuit Conference of Asia Pacific, "About the Jesuits," accessed October 26, 2013, http://sjapc.net/about-us/about-jesuits.
3. Giguère.

CHAPTER TWO
1. Ellen H. Walworth, *The Life and Times of Kateri Tekakwitha: The Lily of the Mohawks 1656–1680* (Buffalo, N.Y.: Peter Paul & Brother, 1891), p. 196.
2. Erik R. Seeman, *The Huron-Wendat Feast: of the Dead: Indian–European Encounters in Early North American* (Baltimore: Johns Hopkins University Press, 2011), p. 52.

CHAPTER THREE
1. Serra to Father Francesch Serra, Aug. 20, 1749, Cádiz, in Tibesar, *Writings of Serra*, 1:5, as quoted in Steven W. Hackel, *Junípero Serra: California's Founding Father* (New York: Hill and Wang, 2013), p. 221.
2. Matthew Bunson et al., eds. *John Paul II's Book of Saints* (Huntington, Ind.: Our Sunday Visitor, 1999), p. 214.
3. Diego de Córdova Salinas, *Crónica franciscana de las provincias del Perú*, ed. Lino Gómez Canedo (Washington, D.C.: Academy of American Franciscan History, 1957), p. 552, as quoted in Hackel, p. 34.

4. William B. Taylor, *Magistrates of the Sacred: Priests and Parishioners in Eighteenth-Century Mexico* (Stanford, Calif.: Stanford University Press, 1996), pp. 216 and 642, n. 62, as quoted in Hackel, p. 86.

CHAPTER FOUR

1. Anne Seton to Weis, as quoted in Annabelle M. Melville, *Elizabeth Bayley Seton: 1774–1821* (New York: Charles Scribner's Sons, 1951), p. 161.
2. Emily Dickinson, "Because I could not stop for Death," *The Complete Poems of Emily Dickinson*, ed. Thomas H. Johnson (Boston: Little, Brown and Company, 1960).
3. Anne Seton, as quoted in Melville, p. 104.
4. Anne Seton to Brute, as quoted in Melville, p. 104.
5. Melville, p. 103.
6. Melville, p. 237.
7. Simon, Bruté's eulogy on Sister Maria Burke, as quoted in Melville, p. 232.
8. Jay P. Dolan, *The American Catholic Experience: A History from Colonial Times to the Present* (Garden City, N.Y.: Doubleday, 1985), p. 121.
9. Melville, pp. 226–227.
10. Anne Seton to Filicchi, April 18, 1820, as quoted in Melville, p. 294.
11. Sr. Marie Celeste, S.C., *The Intimate Friendships of Elizabeth Ann Bayley Seton: First Native Born American Saint (1774–1821)* (New York: Alba House, 1989), p. 18.

CHAPTER FIVE

1. Louise Callan, R.S.C.J., *Philippine Duchesne: Frontier Missionary of the Sacred Heart 1769–1852*, abr. ed. (Westminster, Md.: Newman, 1965; repr., Society of the Sacred Heart, United States Province, 2002), p. 70. Emphasis in original.
2. Callan, p. 427.
3. Callan, p. 22.
4. Callan, p. 76.
5. Callan, p. 103.
6. Catherine M. Mooney, *Philippine Duchesne: A Woman with the Poor* (Eugene, Oreg.: Wipf & Stock, 2007), p. 128.
7. Mooney, p. 127.
8. Callan, p. 432.
9. Callan, p. 487.

CHAPTER SIX

1. Penny Blaker Mitchell, *Mother Theodore Guerin—Saint of God: A Woman for All Time*, p. 181.
2. Katherine Burton, *The Eighth American Saint: The Life of Saint Mother Theodore Guérin, Foundress of the Sisters of Providence of Saint Mary-of-the-Woods, Indiana* (Chicago: ACTA, 2006), p. 51.
3. Burton, *The Eighth American Saint*, p. 68.
4. Burton, *The Eighth American Saint*, p. 80.
5. Burton, *The Eighth American Saint*, p. 262.

6. Burton, *The Eighth American Saint*, p. 98.
7. Mitchell, p. 153.
8. Mitchell, p. 83.
9. Burton, *The Eighth American Saint*, p. 230.
10. Burton, *The Eighth American Saint*, p. 214.
11. Mitchell, p. 177.

CHAPTER SEVEN
1. Richard A. Boever, C.SS.R., Ph.D., *Saint John Neumann: His Writings and Spirituality* (Liguori, Mo.: Liguori, 2010), p. 131.
2. John Neumann, C.SS.R., *The Autobiography of St. John Neumann, C.SS.R*, trans. and commentary by Alfred C. Rush, C.SS.R. (Boston: St. Paul, 1977), p. 17.
3. Neumann, p. 18.
4. Neumann, p. 19.
5. Neumann, p. 27.
6. James J. Galvin, C.SS.R, *Saint John Neumann: Fourth Bishop of Philadelphia* (Baltimore: Helicon, 1977), p. 96.
7. Quoted in William M. Shea, *The Lion and the Lamb: Evangelicals and Catholics in America* (New York: Oxford University Press, 2004), p. 61. Emphasis in original.
8. Richard A. Boever, C.SS.R., Ph.D., "The Spirituality of St. John Neumann," *The Redemptorist North American Historical Bulletin* 12 (1999), p. 11.
9. Galvin, p. 127.
10. Galvin, p. 168.
11. Galvin, p. 192.
12. Neumann, p. 44.

CHAPTER EIGHT
1. "Wise Words of Francis Xavier Seelos," accessed October 26, 2013, http://www.seelos.org/lifeWritings.html.
2. Michael J. Curley, C.SS.R, *Cheerful Ascetic: The Life of Francis Xavier Seelos, C.SS.R.*, 2nd ed. (New Orleans: The Redemptorists, Seelos Center, 2002), p. 21.
3. Curley, p. 48.
4. Curley, p. 66.
5. Curley, p. 72.
6. Curley, p. 134.
7. Curley, p. 139.
8. Curley, p. 181.
9. Curley, p. 198.
10. Curley, p. 199.
11. Curley, p. 214.
12. Curley, p. 225.

CHAPTER NINE
1. Letter from Damien to his parents, January 16, 1861, as quoted in Gavan Daws, *Holy Man: Father Damien of Molokai* (Honolulu: University of Hawaii Press, 1973), p. 28.
2. Koeckemann to Raepsaet, July 27, 1891, as quoted in Daws, p. 241.
3. Fouesnel to Bousquet, November 16, 1883, as quoted in Daws, p. 120.
4. Typescript by Dutton, as quoted in Daws, p. 248.
5. Daws, p. 24.
6. Damien to Pamphile, August 23, 1864, as quoted in Daws, p. 37.
7. Damien, May 28, 1873, as quoted in Daws, p. 83.
8. Anwei Skinsnes Law and Henry G. Law, *Father Damien...A Bit of Taro, A Piece of Fish, and A Glass of Water* (Seneca Falls, N.Y.: IDEA Center for the Voices of Humanity, 2009), p. 10.
9. *Pacific Commercial Advertiser,* June 14, 1873, as quoted in Daws, p. 64.
10. Daws, p. 86.
11. Ambrose Hutchison, as quoted in Daws, p. 113.

CHAPTER TEN
1. Sr. Mary Laurence Hanley, O.S.F. and O.A. Bushnell, *Pilgrimage and Exile: Mother Marianne of Molokai,* rev. ed. (Honolulu: Mutual, 2009), p. 288.
2. Hanley and Bushnell, p. 28.
3. Hanley and Bushnell, p. 34.
4. Daws, p. 126.
5. Hanley and Bushnell, p. 87.
6. Hanley and Bushnell, p. 285.

CHAPTER ELEVEN
1. Frances X. Cabrini, *To the Ends of the Earth: The Missionary Travels of Frances X. Cabrini,* trans. Philippa Provenzano, M.S.C. (New York: Center for Migration Studies, 2001), p. xx.
2. Mother Saverio de Maria, M.S.C., *Mother Frances Xavier Cabrini,* Rose Basile Green, trans. (Chicago: Missionary Sisters of the Sacred Heart of Jesus, 1984), p. 16.
3. De Maria, p. 261
4. De Maria, p. 43.
5. De Maria, p. 54
6. De Maria, p. 79.
7. De Maria, p. 86.
8. De Maria, p. 96.
9. Cabrini, p. xvii.
10. De Maria, p. 112.
11. De Maria, pp. 159–160.
12. De Maria, p. 230.
13. Letter written on ship from New York to Nicaragua, October 1891, Cabrini, p. 49.
14. Letter from Chicago, February 1906, Cabrini, p. 282.

15. Letter written on ship from Genoa to New York, September 1894, Cabrini, p. 81.
16. Letter written on ship from Liverpool to New York, November 1889, Cabrini, p. 192.
17. Letter written on ship from Genoa to Buenos Aires, December 1900, Cabrini, p. 217.

CHAPTER TWELVE

1. Lou Baldwin, *Saint Katharine Drexel: Apostle to the Oppressed* (Philadelphia: The Catholic Standard and Times, 2000), p. 58.
2. Positio, as quoted in Baldwin, p. 196.
3. Katherine Burton, *The Golden Door: The Life of Katharine Drexel* (New York: P.J. Kenedy & Sons, 1957), p. 217.
4. Baldwin, p. 42.
5. Sr. Consuela Marie Duffy, S.B.S., as quoted in Baldwin, p. 37.
6. Bishop O'Connor to Katharine Drexel, as quoted in Baldwin, p. 58.
7. Baldwin, p. 2.
8. Burton, *The Golden Door*, p. 100.
9. Duffy, p. 151, as quoted in Baldwin, p. 82.
10. ASBS, v. 3, p. 110, as quoted in Baldwin, p. 89.
11. Burton, *The Golden Door*, pp. 189–190.
12. Burton, *The Golden Door,* pp. 231–233.
13. Burton, *The Golden Door,* p. 249.
14. ASBS, vs. 26, p. 225, as quoted in Baldwin, p. 167.
15. Burton, *The Golden Door,* p. 275.
16. Duffy, p. 371, as quoted in Baldwin, p. 188.
17. Burton, *The Golden Door*, p. 293.

About the Authors

Alice Camille is a writer, religious educator, and parish retreat leader who received a Master of Divinity degree from the Franciscan School of Theology in Berkeley. She has authored nine books, numerous articles and regular columns, writes the monthly commentary "Exploring the Sunday Readings" and has helped develop catechetical materials for schools and parishes.

Paul Boudreau is a priest of the Diocese of Norwich, Connecticut, and is pastor at St. Mary's Church in Portland, Connecticut. He is the author of *Between Sundays: Daily Gospel Reflections and Prayers*, and has written many articles on various aspects of parish and pastoral ministry.